ENDORSEMENTS

All of humanity lives with God-given purpose. Without purpose, humanity cannot live as God intended. *Reignite* is a practical guide to living out your purpose as God intended from the inside out. Written from the heart of God, you will be encouraged to know you are uniquely loved by God, challenged to walk by faith and not by sight, and given practical tools to deal with the roadblocks that hinder destiny.

Abner Suarez
International Speaker and Author
Creation Reborn: Your Invitation to God's Divine Design
Dunn, NC

Natasha Tubbs has hit the ball out of the park. You can literally feel through every sentence the breath of God and the wind of the Holy Spirit reigniting us to stay the course and not give up. *Reignite* reminds the reader that every single one of us was called for a specific purpose. The fact of the matter is that we are HIS WORKMANSHIP. It is not ours to determine our own destiny, nor the worlds, nor that of enemies. Our Creator has prepared good works in advance for us to accomplish, and He has also wired us so intricately in order to fulfill those things. But, not so fast, she reminds us that the enemy of our soul also has specific plans for our lives, and his job is to blow out the fire of destiny and purpose in our lives so we will end up drifting far away from God's original intent. She gives us keys, using her own personal experiences on how to tightly hang on through the storms of life while holding onto God and never allowing any wind of darkness nor discouragement to blow us off course so that we drift away. Natasha also encourages us that if our fire has been snuffed out because of life's hard knocks, it's never too late. The fire of purpose can be REIGNITED!!!

Maria Durso
Speaker and Author
From Your Head to Your Heart:
The Change You Long for is 18 Inches Away
New York City, NY

Reignite takes you on a beautiful journey that guides the reader from theory to action in a practical yet Biblically-sound manner. By sharing from her own personal journey with God, Natasha's style of writing feels like words coming from a friend full of truth and a touch of sass. The themes of living by bold faith and overcoming obstacles are intricately woven into this book, and I am encouraged and inspired by Natasha's honesty and transparency. When you find a book like this that gives you spiritual insight in a thought-provoking manner, you get a cup of your favorite coffee or tea, find a comfortable spot and delve into it. You will be empowered, equipped, and full of zeal to live ignited for God after you read this book.

Mercy Lokulutu
Speaker and Author
As You Wish: Finding True Strength in Surrender to God
Dallas, TX

Natasha Tubbs' book, *Reignite*, is destined to become a mainstay in the earnest Christian's resource library. Natasha dives into the urgent matter of sustaining a passionate relationship with God and focused life-purpose with candor, courage, and challenge. Expect to be engaged and surprised—Natasha doesn't depend on overused jargon or Christian cliché for one moment. *Reignite's* generous layers of scripture reiterate the wisdom found on every page resulting in a riveting impartation. No matter one's flame-status, prepare to be stoked!

Tava Brice
International Speaker and Women's Ministry Leader
Covenant Love Church
Fayetteville, NC

Wow! Thank you for releasing this timely message! *Reignite* is the perfect follow up to Natasha's book *In Pursuit of Purpose*. This book has inspired me and given me practical tools to keep walking in my God-given destiny. I love the balance of Biblical truth, sports analogies, and Natasha's transparency. *Reignite* is a must-read for anyone that desires to live a life of significance.

Brian Chu
Global Missionary
Now Hope
Colorado Springs, Colorado

REIGNITE

Awakening the Fire Within When Life Threatens to Extinguish It

NATASHA TUBBS

UNITED HOUSE

Re-

(Prefix) again: anew [1]

Ignite

ig·nite \ ig-ˈnīt \

(Verb) To subject to fire or intense heat; *especially*:
to render luminous by heat [2]

UNITED HOUSE Publishing
Waterford, Michigan
info@unitedhousepublishing.com
www.unitedhousepublishing.com

Cover and Interior Design: Matt Russell, Marketing Image, mrussell@marketing-image.com
Cover Image Design: Ronald Spatafore, ronaldspatafore.com

Printed in the United States of America
2019—First Edition

SPECIAL SALES
Most UNITED HOUSE books are available at special quantity discounts when purchased in bulk by corporations, organizations, and special-interest groups. For information, please e-mail orders@unitedhousepublishing.com

I dedicate this book to those who are courageous enough to walk on the stormy seas of life. Those who believe they were created for more than existence. Although the waters of life arise and threaten to drown out the faith alive on the inside, they hold firm to God's words that whisper to their soul, "Trust Me."

CONTENTS

FOREWORD

One of the greatest issues facing the Church today is one of "identity"—meaning who we are in Christ Jesus. One of the most impacting statements I have heard in recent years concerning this was, "What we *behold*—we become." As Christians, we must understand how we behold—or see our Father God, directly impacts how we see ourselves as a son or daughter of God and therefore significantly impacts the way in which we walk through this world. It is crucial for Christians today to understand the truth concerning how to "behold Jesus"—to see their identity in Christ Jesus. We need to see ourselves as complete and whole in Him—not lacking in or wanting for anything. Matthew 5:48 (ESV) instructs us, "You therefore must be perfect, as your heavenly Father is perfect." This does not mean we are *perfect* in the sense of never sinning or making a mistake. The word here for perfect means *complete*. This means perfect in the sense that we are *complete* in Christ Jesus!

Over the last few years in the medical world of the US Military, a new therapy originated for treating veterans who had lost a limb due to combat trauma. This unique therapy is called "Mirror Therapy." This particular type of physical therapy has the veteran place a mirror up to the area next to where a limb was lost. For instance, if the veteran's right arm was lost, he would stand with his right side against the mirror. As he looks at himself in the mirror, what he observes is the image of his left arm appearing as a restored "right arm." Each time he moves his left arm during physical therapy, he sees his "right arm" moving again. Now, instead of having a self-image of being broken or incomplete, the veteran now sees himself as whole. He begins to have a totally different view of himself. This therapy has been proven to be highly successful in the healing process.

We are living in a day and time in which readers seem to be satisfied with various Christian authors merely offering another pseudo-psychological self-help book with catchphrases meant for sound bites or posts on social media which really offer no significant Biblical truth. I can assure you, this book is not one of those! What Natasha is offering you in her new book *Reignite* is an opportunity based upon the solid foundation of scriptural truth, to see yourself as a whole. She is offering each reader an opportunity to behold God in His true character and nature as our Father—and to see beyond their current situation into the truth of what God says about them.

Natasha is not offering you a bottle of the *milk* of the Word—this is truly fine dining on the *meat* of the Word which will challenge you to believe God with a new depth of relationship and purpose. A depth of faith that goes beyond seeing what you need to see yourself in a place where you have everything you need to live a victorious life in Christ Jesus! As Natasha states, "Our identity as His children is what gives us **purpose** to fulfill the destiny He created us each for." Natasha will also challenge you into a new place of deep self-reflection and will challenge the ways you've previously thought about and approached circumstances and situations in your life. As she transparently shares some of her journey, you will understand you must no longer stand amid the storms of life overwhelmed and afraid, but instead, are able to walk through storms with new confidence and faith because of your identity in Jesus knowing what He has already done and is doing on your behalf.

Because I've known Natasha for years and because I've watched her walk through what she is teaching in this book, I know one of the greatest desires of her heart is to help you walk in your identity and purpose. You are about to read a book that will challenge you to a new level of faith—true faith in Jesus and completeness in the truth of the identity He has given you. So, even if there is now just an ember in your heart—let the Spirit of God use *Reignite* to fan it into a burning flame and illuminate your identity and purpose in Jesus!

Dr. David W. Mosher
School of Ministry, Senior Leader
Covenant Love Church, Fayetteville NC

INTRODUCTION

Have you ever come face to face with your own faith? I am talking the ultimate crossroad in your faith where you must choose between the wild adventure of walking with Jesus or staying in the monotony of where you are! Well, these are the very stories that fill the Bible that we read each and every single day. Real women and men like you and me who came face to face with who they were created to be. From walking on the waves of a wild storm like Peter, as Jesus beckoned him to come, to being delivered by the Lord from ravishing flames, like Shadrach, Meshach, and Abednego, as they stood upon the foundation of their faith. But, the story of the Samaritan Woman is one in particular which always quickens my soul. Why? Because this story encapsulates the beautiful theme hidden in each and every story that we and the characters of the Bible faced: Jesus is determined to see us come to know the Father and become all He desires us to be. And, through the revelation of our true identity, we would live lives that reveal the character and nature of our Father in heaven. Not for us to live up to the title of "Christian," but to be His.

In chapter four of the book of John, Jesus goes out of His way to encounter this woman at the well, who by society's standards, was found to be unworthy. The road He chose to meet her on was opposite a path intentionally created to avoid the town this woman belonged to; the town of Samaria. But, Jesus was led by the Holy Spirit through this forgotten place instead of around it. [3] He did not shy away and go the other way. Jesus was determined to encounter her! He did not settle for political correctness but approached her stirred by love and compassion. He knew something this woman did not know: She was meant for so much more than she was living.

Jesus's utterance to the heart of this Samaritan woman at the well reveals what the life of a disciple should look like: "a fresh, bubbling spring" (John 4:14), lives meant to refresh the lives of others. This was God Almighty's plan for this woman, beyond where she had been living. He craved to see her freed from her sin and her shame and to fulfill her purpose; to know and be known by the God of the universe. Her destiny was to fulfill His wonderful plans that would reveal His majesty in the earth. And we, my friends, like that Samaritan woman, were created for the same.

My prayer and mission for *Reignite* is that it will not just be a challenge to every person to go beyond being content and remaining in their comfort zone; but that it will be a complete shift in thought patterns. That it will be food for those who hunger and thirst for righteousness. That as the body of Christ, we will "press on" together as the apostle Paul says in Philippians 3:14, toward the call of expanding the kingdom of God in the earth.

I wholeheartedly believe that as disciples of Jesus Christ, we all must get to the place where we are willing to go beyond the shore of comfort and into the depths of where God is calling us to. We were meant to have vibrant and heaven-revealing lives reflecting His Kingdom. We were created to live like springs that never run dry because the Creator of the universe dwells on the inside of our hearts. Similar to the woman at the well who encountered Jesus, we also have the choice to take that bold step of faith and pursue all God has in store for our lives, no matter what comes our way, or remain in the comfort of where we have always been.

I pray that through these pages you will become fully awakened to the race that is ahead: the marathon of life that calls each of us to be fully alive in Christ Jesus. Through the ups and downs of this earthly life, that you would remain like a brightly burning fire that never goes out! The time has come to kick the dust off our feet and run the great race and fight the great fight of faith for which you and I were created. No matter what this season looks like, I pray that the fire within your soul is REIGNITED by the Holy Spirit to not only run the race but finish strong!

PART ONE

As children of God, many elements can contribute to the fires of our souls growing dim. In order to *run the race*, as the Apostle Paul says (Philippians 3:14), we must comprehend the part we play. Until we gain the revelation of who we are, we miss out on accomplishing all which God desires for us. In the first part of this book, we'll learn how to recognize our identity in Christ in order to equip us to move forward in our individual destinies.

1

ENDURE THE RACE

I admit I am a bit of an app (application) addict. I have an app on my cell phone for just about everything! When I need to grocery shop, I log on to my grocery app, make my list, set up a time for pick-up, then I show up at my scheduled time to the store, and my groceries are put into the trunk of my car. When I want a quick lunch, I hop on my app, order, then pick it up. This goes for coffee, breakfast, even clothes shopping! This is the benefit of living in an "order ahead" culture. Don't get me wrong, convenience is EVERYTHING to me. With a large family like mine, dragging four humans who have their own plans inside of anywhere could make my trip much longer than expected. So, I am all for convenience! But with all things, wisdom tells us to be mindful to balance our need for convenience. As God's children, if we don't live in balance, we can begin to treat our whole lives—including our destiny—in ways which cause us to search for shortcuts to our final destination to fit our desire for convenience.

God gave me a great illustration of this one day in my quiet time.

Picture this: You wake up one day, ready to get your day started, and out of the corner of your eye, something grabs your attention. On your nightstand, you find a beautiful box and a handwritten card from God himself which reads:

"Your hand-crafted destiny inside."
~Sincerely,
God: The Father, Jesus, and the Holy Spirit
XOXO

Wouldn't it be nice if life were this easy? Wouldn't it be great if we woke up one day with a gift-wrapped box from God which included a detailed list of our destiny and what we'd need to do in order to fulfill it? But what God revealed to me was, if I had a box which held the details to my destiny, I wouldn't pursue Him intimately or intentionally. I am not going to pretend; I would love it if our whole lives were delivered in a box! We would completely avoid making choices which could hinder our future (or any choices for that matter). In fact, we wouldn't have the opportunity to experience anything, including the scariest thing ever: Failure. The point I want to make is this: God desires for us to realize that clinging to ease would leave out important elements of our (sometimes messy) journey. God intended the path to discovering our purpose to be a journey we'd walk (or take) with Him.

We can rejoice, too, when we run into problems and
trials, for we know that they help us develop endurance.
And endurance develops strength of character,
and character strengthens our confident hope of
salvation. And this hope will not lead to disappointment.
For we know how dearly God loves us, because
he has given us the Holy Spirit to fill our
hearts with his love.
Romans 5:3-5

This exhortation encourages us to rejoice, even if we don't possess all the answers to our future. Because when we do hold on, we endure for the long haul, instead of settling for shortcuts. I have been guilty of looking for shortcuts in life. Getting to the finish line is much more appetizing than running the race. Running the full competition requires you to be stretched beyond your comfort. Sure, we can run, at our own speed, in our own time. But, we are talking about real-life here! Real-life rarely goes according to plan, whether we like it or not. This is the exact point I spoke of before where many of us may have missed it. Shortcuts never get us the full result we would have received had we done things the "right" way. When we attempt to run the race of faith on our own terms of ease and comfort, we miss the mark. This is why I am always stirred when the Apostle Paul reminds us to:

Press on to reach the end of the race and receive the heavenly prize for which God, through Christ Jesus, is calling us.
Philippians 3:14

When we choose to press on through the inconvenience, and the times we just wish would end, even though it may seem pointless, our character truly reflects His! Why?

Endurance develops strength of character, and character strengthens our confident hope of salvation.
Romans 5:4

In the middle of the greatest fight of our lives, it can be easy to say nevermind to the hope that we will ever get through it. But, Romans 5:4 offers us a perspective that there *is* something to look forward to, even in the midst of those seasons. Hope says we *can* get through the storm. Hope says we *are* rooted in Jesus. Hope says it is *not* over! We only need to keep moving!

PRESS ON

Have you ever participated or competed in a sport? Throughout my childhood up until my first year in college, I played in competitive leagues. I played a bit of soccer, spent time playing basketball but found my niche in volleyball. In each sport, there was just something about the challenge that always drew me in for more! And so, naturally, growing up, Philippians 3:14 was always one of my favorite Scriptures. It offers this great revelation while comparing it to something we can easily all relate to, running a race. Whether you have run for a competitive track team or raced to catch your dog who slipped loose from its leash, we have all had to run with everything we've got! And so, I have always loved this Scripture because, from a modern-day perspective, it reads like an encouraging chant, like the one that might be heard right before an athletic event. It is a call to victory to those about to embark on the greatest race of their life! Because let's face it, we all need to be encouraged (and reminded) sometimes to "press on."

When I think back, one of my favorite occasions in athletic events has always been the moment where the coach and the team come together for a team-building chant to get the minds of each player ready for what is ahead. It is a time to focus on the goal of the event; a successful finish. This passage, in particular, compares the journey of life to a race, complete with a successful finish as its goal.

Anyone who has ever run a race knows full well it will require intensive training. A race is not a "just show up" kind of experience. A runner must know their course well. They must eat, sleep, and train hard. There is no way to finish well without preparation and determination. Settling for less will not do. In comparison, this journey of life will require the very same tenacity.

Personally, I love the opportunity to be challenged. For this reason,

I love sports and growing up, I played basketball and volleyball competitively. In case you didn't notice, running is not listed as one of my beloved favorites! These days, my sport of choice is weightlifting. I love the challenge to stretch, define, and tone my muscles. While on the other hand, I always felt like running was just not the challenge I, nor my body, enjoyed. In my mind, running makes me feel like I am dying when I expect to be feeling good. I am confident if I spent more time doing it, and challenging myself in it, I would enjoy it like I enjoy weightlifting (eventually). This is what I think of when I take a look back at the passage in Philippians 3.

The training and challenges which running the race of life presents will require more than just showing up. Even more, like running a race, there is an awareness of the destination, but how long it takes to run our race will vary in our willingness to press on and give ourselves over to the process. Only faithful endurance will determine true success. Some days it will seem so hard, you will feel like giving up. But you know you won't, because the destination is worth the cost. Now let's take a moment to go back and walk through the Philippians 3 passage step-by-step because I don't want us to miss the revelation it offers:

> *Press on to reach the end of the race and receive*
> *the heavenly prize for which God, through Christ*
> *Jesus, is calling us.*
> *Philippians 3:14*

The Apostle Paul challenges the reader to "press on." Throughout this life, we have all been faced with circumstances which require us to stay on the path. On occasion, those circumstances do not always feel good. And in the midst of those times, the last thing you want to do is keep going! But, if we compare life to running a race, we are able to understand what Paul was getting at. As with any long-distance race, the finish line is not within an arm's reach. It is far off and will require you to push yourself and test your ability to get there. When you feel like you have nothing left, you will have to "press on" to reach the end. You will have to pursue the finish line as if your life depended on it.

Marathoners are conditioned in this way to run very long distances. They are trained to understand hard work is ahead of them. The distance is predetermined and is the same length for every person who runs it: 26.2 miles. All of the contenders complete the same trek. The qualification of the runner does not shorten or lengthen the distance of the race. However, it is the runner's determination and preparation or lack thereof which defines the time it will take for them to reach the finish line. So also, we, as children of God, runners in the race of life, must be proactively running toward the prize awaiting us. Not in the escape of this world, but as lights on a hill pressing forward until we reach our destination (Matthew 5:14).

In December 2017, I finished a race I had been running for a long time, earning my second graduate degree. After ten years of education (beyond high school), I finally finished a season I had worked very hard to complete. I began my bachelor's degree program right out of high school, but it was delayed because I met my husband, and we had our first son. When our son was two, my husband joined the Army, then we had our only girl. When she was about one, I decided to go back to college and complete my bachelor's. Fast forward ten years, we had two more sons, and I had a total of three degrees. Trust me, it would be quite easy to brag about accomplishments, but I know for a fact, none of it was easy.

Every single program stretched me beyond my comfort zone. I was taught and untaught many things. I faced rejection, disagreement, and I often felt isolated. But between moving across the country several times, giving birth, and countless life events, I crossed the finish line, and I am thankful. The journey of pressing on when I wanted to quit taught me there is much more inside of me than I could have ever imagined. Sure, I have degrees to show for my work, but I have knowledge, persistence, and endurance to show for my willingness to press on through to the end.

Let's jump back to the passage. Next, we see there is a "heavenly prize" awaiting at the end of the race of life:

> **Press on to reach the end of the race and**
> **receive the heavenly prize...**
> **Philippians 3:14**

As children of God, we are pressing on to the finish line of heaven! We know as children of God, this is our future. But just like a marathon runner, we have to train and stretch ourselves to arrive there. As long as we continue running, we will reach our destination. The place where we get distracted as Christians is when we settle for less and don't value the journey because we view "arriving in heaven" as the only reward. The Bible shows us time and time again this race is so much more.

Just as no true athlete runs a race simply for the prize, we also are called to run the race of life with more in mind than the destination. Athletes who play sports do not train until their hands hurt or their feet bleed for a trophy or their name on a plaque. (Neither do those who study hard for years on end do so simply for the sake of saying they did.) No! It is the joy of completion after achieving their goal. It is the overwhelming sense of accomplishment in a task which many give up on every single day. It is the tested and true fact they have endured until the end.

As children of God, we must run the race of life with the same commitment as any tried and true athlete. We must press on because there is much more at stake than our entrance into Heaven. Jesus died so no person would perish (John 3:16). We live in a world of perpetual darkness where there are men and women dying daily and spending eternity without Heaven because, often, we who are called to be the example of endurance have become consumed with punching our ticket to heaven rather than seeing other souls set free. Jesus left us with the Great Commission for a reason. Please don't misunderstand me! Heaven is our great gift and inheritance as children of God. But it not our mission in this life. Our mission is the same one which Jesus gave to His disciples:

> *Go therefore and make disciples of all the nations, baptizing them in the name of the Father and of the Son and of the Holy Spirit.*
> *Matthew 28:19 NKJV*

Running the race has never been about works or lack thereof. It has always been about seeing those who are enslaved are set free. Our race as children of God is a forward-moving progression to more free people and fewer slaves in this world. I believe we are in a day and age where the commission to see disciples made of all nations is more alive than it has ever been in any other time. I say this because there is more access to the Gospel than ever before. People all around the world can access the Gospel for free through Bibles, tablets, cell phones, etc. Even where feet cannot reach, people are sharing what Jesus has done in their lives. This is why we run the race. This is our cause!

OUR GOD-GIVEN MANDATE

The cause of Christ, to see slaves of sin set free, is our mandate. We do not run this race in vain for a ticket to Heaven but because we are a part of accomplishing the work on earth which Christ began! We should not be Heaven chasers but eternity sealers. We should be so busy about the Father's business that getting to Heaven is like the cherry on top of an ice-cream sundae. The difference between those who walk through life with contentment and those who don't will come down to one specific thing, believing you were created for more. *Ponder on this.*

Walking in our destiny as children of God will not look like it does in the world around us. Countercultural living already puts us in the position to stand out. We have a different perspective and set of beliefs, but just because it is an uncommon way to live, does not mean it is impossible. Jesus said it best when discussing the possibility of salvation with His disciples:

Humanly speaking, it is impossible.
But with God everything is possible.
Matthew 19:26b

Regardless of what others think about your journey, the grace you need to run the race of life will be there as you step into unity with the Father. We are never alone in this process. In every difficulty we face, God is right there strengthening and working through us to help us endure.

For God is working in you, giving you the desire
and the power to do what pleases Him.
Philippians 2:13

The pressing on which we each have to do will look different. Nevertheless, we all have access to the same Spirit to help us and are all commissioned and headed in the same direction.

I remember the times in my life where I questioned my direction, times where I was worried I would never be able to catch up to other Christians. I wrestled with the verse in Philippians of God working in me. I worried I would never become the person I needed to be to merit an entrance into Heaven. But, it was only when I truly encountered Jesus, when I began to understand the *actual* gospel. He showed me that grace in my life was never based on my merit. He taught me about having a Kingdom-mindset which, as a child of the King, continually confirms my destination will always be an eternity with Him. The more time I spent with Jesus, the more I learned I am righteous because of His works, not my own:

> **We are made right with God by placing our faith**
> **in Jesus Christ. And this is true for everyone**
> **who believes, no matter who we are.**
> **Romans 3:22**

During one season in particular, things had gotten really busy in my life, and I began to burn out. There was a great demand for me and my time. I found it frustrating. I couldn't just sit with Jesus for an hour and dote on Him. I began to complain and pity myself for not having the time I "wanted." I began to criticize myself in prayer to God (yes, it is possible) about how sorry I was for not "doing" enough. Suddenly, out of nowhere, the Holy Spirit spoke to my heart.

In that instant, I got a wakeup call as the Holy Spirit spoke to my heart. Now, in theory, we know the Holy Spirit is ministering to our hearts all of the time, but often we forget. He is never silent. Sometimes, we are just not listening. Whether I was listening or not, He grabbed my attention.

As clear as I can hear my own thoughts, I heard the Holy Spirit say, "You could never do enough." At first, I was offended and thought it had to be Satan because of how I felt about this response. But then He repeated, "You could never do enough." This time, my heart instantly softened and quieted within me. I perceived He didn't mean spiritual disciplines like reading the word and prayer were wrong. Rather, He was correcting my perspective of righteousness. He was reminding me I am righteous because of what Jesus has done. By my faith in Him, I am seen as right in the Father's eyes. So instead of trying to "work" myself into God's good favor, I get to "be" in relationship with Him. This is the eternity we have the privilege to hide within our hearts. Our reward isn't hidden in doing things *for* Jesus, but *being in* Him for eternity.

Like a beautiful garden waiting to burst into vibrant colors at the beginning of spring, God has already planted such things in us:

> *He has made everything beautiful in its time.*
> *Also He has put eternity in their hearts,*
> *except that no one can find out the work*
> *that God does from beginning to end.*
> *Ecclesiastes 3:11 NKJV*

With this eternal mindset—knowing we are forever citizens of God's Kingdom and righteous in Christ—our souls begin to bloom with purpose as we journey towards all which God has planned for us since before He formed the ground we walk on.

Until we are grounded *on* our identity, we cannot walk fully into our destiny. We must know and embrace this truth: As Christians, we are now the righteousness of God because of Jesus. This means we aren't working to constantly earn right-standing before God. No. The gospel says in Christ, we are right with God.

The journey on Earth isn't about us striving toward a position. Jesus earned and gave us this position, and now part of our destiny is to tell others it is available to them. As this revelation is cemented in our souls, a holy fire is reignited in our hearts and the passion of Heaven beckons us into our calling.

2

Provoke The Faith Within

There once was a man who prayed earnestly for a vehicle, and he received exactly what he requested. The problem was, what he received was not *really* what he'd envisioned. He sought God for a vehicle to get him where he needed to go. What he got was a bicycle. Yes, it moved him from point A to point B, and a bicycle *is* a great mode of transportation but only in desirable weather. One cannot comfortably ride a bicycle in rain or snow. It can be done, but it is not advisable. When he asked God why He blessed him with a bicycle and not a car, God answered, "You did not ask for a car."

Regrettably, I can relate to this man. In the past, instead of asking God *in faith* for what I needed, instead, I complained when I got what I did pray for. My experience may differ a bit from the man in the story, but the lesson I learned is the same.

When we moved to Hawaii, we were away from our church home (4,700 miles to be exact). I was looking for a way to connect to a group of women who loved Jesus as I did. Instead of asking for this, when I sought God, I prayed, "God send me women to hang out with." He answered. And, boy, did I meet ladies; quite a few actually. One detail I neglected to pray for (mostly because I had no idea of how to ask), was for them to be women who loved Him. There is just a special feel to a relationship when you are both head over heels for Jesus!

I found early on that each new woman I met, although great mothers and wives, were just not what I needed. One day in prayer, I asked the Lord why I wasn't making Godly girlfriends; the kind of friends who just minster right into your season of life. The type of friends who bless you because of who they are in Christ. And the Holy Spirit answered as He pointed me right to Scripture:

> **You ask and do not receive, because you**
> **ask wrongly, to spend it on your passions.**
> **James 4:3 ESV**

Yikes! I was so desperate for friends to fill my time within the new season of my life, I forgot to seek God for what He had for me. It became very clear that I didn't just need people fillers to make me feel comfortable. God created you and me for more than that. He created us for community! And so, He revealed not just any group of ladies would meet the need I had of that community. I quickly aligned my thoughts with God and sought Him for what I truly needed: women who loved Him, as I did.

This situation also revealed something deep inside that the Father wanted to shift in me. A new perspective was needed. One that would challenge me to step into territory that I had only read about in the Bible and would stretch me further to utilize my faith. The current perspective I had revealed that I didn't yet believe God would give me the desires of my heart (a community of like-minded women). And so, I needed to hope for more. And all of that changed with prayer.

Because He is a loving Father, He led me to not only pray in faith but to pray specifically; I asked God to lead me to women who were involved in a Bible study and would invite me to join. Not only did God hear my faith-filled prayer, but He answered it within days. At my daughter's next ballet practice, I met a woman who invited me to a military wives' Bible study called PWOC (Protestant Women of the Chapel). And not only did she invite me, but she was a new Christian! God sent a new believer to this self-declared "mature" believer to get me connected in fellowship. I learned pretty quickly, God does answer the prayers we pray!

If we are honest, instead of asking God for things in faith, we occasionally turn to complaining. When grumbling becomes a pattern, we can start falsely believing if we complain long enough, it will entice Him to do what we want. This perspective reminds me of spoiled children who whine when things aren't going their way or feel like they are missing out on the "best things" in life. But this is not the identity of God's faithful ones who trust in Him. God's expectations of His children are of trust and purpose. Therefore, asking in faith is a regular display of trust in our Father. It is this hope-filled praying which causes the flame of faith to burn bright in some and stokes the dimly lit fire in others. You could say, asking reveals an intimate trusting relationship between Father and children.

ASK, SEEK, KNOCK

Today, I am a mother of four, filled-to-the-brim, full-of-life children. But before our family became complete with the four, we believed we were complete with only two of them. We had one girl and one boy. According to the rule of 2.5 children, we were complete, or so we thought. As a family, we felt complete (we just had no interest in being the family with the most kids). But like they say, when you make plans, get ready to hear God laugh!

One day, it was almost like the desire to expand our family was rooted in my heart overnight. I went from never wanting more children, to a burning desire for my womb to be filled. I began praying, "God, what is happening? Where is this desire coming from?" And then I knew. He had a special gift for us, another little one. He wanted to bless our family with a child that He had a purpose for. What He had for our family was bigger than our plans and deeper than our imagination. This child was a promise.

Over that next year, the desire continued to grow, but it was taking longer to manifest than I expected. I just knew that if God had given me the desire, it would just happen. I mean, He is God! But that isn't how it happened. Every month I took a pregnancy test. And every single month it ended in the dreaded single line (which as we women know can mean different things in different seasons). To say that I was disappointed was an understatement! I was furious! Furious with my body for not getting the memo. Furious with my husband for not being as obsessed as I was. Furious at God for making me wait! But none of that furious anger frightened or pushed God away. He was ever so patient with me. He's so good!

I learned in that year what it meant to wait on God. My heart ached as I learned that my timing is not His timing. My disappointed hope in the gift I longed for became a heart that was breaking piece-by-piece. "God, how can you do this to me," I cried out as I stared at those tests through blurry eyes. No one knew, other than my husband and I, of the struggle to conceive this promise (that we didn't originally plan for). I mean, how could I possibly explain the anguish I felt as I waited for something I didn't even know I wanted?! Relationship with Jesus, that's how. God used this very unique experience to show me that my faith was fragmented. It was based on what I desired to see in my life, only as I planned it.

By His Holy Spirit, God was drawing me deeper. He was stretching me to pursue His heart and all that came with that journey, past my own plans. As I began moving toward a greater pursuit of His heart for me, He revealed that faith rooted in Him is long-lasting. It doesn't end with a desire but gives us the courage to walk it out until all we hope for comes to pass. Because when He gives us a promise, He always fulfills it (Jeremiah 1:12).

Throughout that very long year, my heart position had shifted from anguish to trusting God. The fruit of trust that was produced in that time multiplied exponentially. I learned that throwing up prayer without expectation was like planting a seed never expecting a harvest. God had challenged me to go further as He expanded my capacity to receive from Him. And in that process of trusting Him, I received those much anticipated two pink lines! As a matter of fact, I was so captivated by the Father, I had almost forgotten to even take a test until our daughter (who was two at the time), said, "Mommy, you have a baby brother in your tummy." Which I brushed off with, "No hunny. Mommy is just bloated." And the promise came flooding back (Spoiler alert: that beautiful baby was a boy!).

Asking. Seeking. Knocking. They are all action verbs that were always meant to compel us to hope, to pursue His heart as we walk it all out in faith. In Scripture, they play a vital role in revealing the endurance of our faith. In particular, Jesus made it very clear how important asking is in our relationship with the Father:

> *If you abide in me, and my words abide in you,*
> *ask whatever you wish, and it will be done for you.*
> *John 15:7 NKJV*

In other words, we come to know who we are in Christ as we spend time in dialogue with the lover of our soul. Through this intimate time we spend in His presence and His Word, we develop faith and boldness to ask with God's perspective in mind. The "Secret Place", as Psalm 91 calls it, gives birth to our purpose as we learn to walk in who we are destined to be. As we aspire to walk authentically in the unique destiny God crafted for our lives, we'll find ourselves complaining less and living lives which inspire others to discover their own purpose. As a matter of fact, we won't complain at all because we would be focused on the journey ahead and not the "have-nots" around us (like I was as I awaited my sweet baby!).

When we set our hearts on the journey of trusting Him, grumbling will be far from our minds. Why? Because when we are focused on our purpose, we know each and every step is vital in moving closer and closer to the future prize. Not for the sake of prizes, but for the sake of being effective. I first learned this truth when my own prayer life wasn't yielding the fruit Jesus communicated to His disciples:

> *Ask, and it will be given to you; seek, and you*
> *will find; knock, and it will be opened to you.*
> *For everyone who asks receives, and he who*
> *seeks finds, and to him who knocks it will be*
> *opened. Or what man is there among you who,*
> *if his son asks for bread, will give him a stone?*
> *Or if he asks for a fish, will he give him a serpent?*
> *If you then, being evil, know how to give good*
> *gifts to your children, how much more will*
> *your Father who is in heaven give good*
> *things to those who ask Him!*
> *Matthew 7:7-11 NKJV*

When we position our hearts to ask, seek, and knock, we are strategically remaining in a position to receive all God desires to communicate to us. So if this method of "ask, seek, and knock" positions our heart to receive, then it would mean anything less could limit our receiving.

Before I understood this truth, I often prayed half-heartedly or I gave up before ever seeing the manifestation of my answered prayer (not always comprehending I was doing so). Prayer at its simplest is just a conversation with God. It is absolutely okay to share about your hurts and struggles, just like you would do with a loved one or friend, and even ask them to be removed. But, in order to pray in faith, you need to understand that God is good and loving, and if He doesn't remove the pain instantly or tells you "no", it is for His greater good in your life. I know I am personally thankful for those "unanswered prayers" - times when God did not give me what I asked for.

Praying in faith means believing that He can do it, and sometimes, He will (backed with what His Word says), but it may not be in the way we thought or on the timeline we hoped for. It is an intentional pursuit of the Father's heart. We cannot manipulate God to do things. Faith is the currency by which God acts. I believe this to be one of the many difficult aspects to learn in today's church because we are in a quick-response age where everything is given, most of the time without hard work or endurance. (thank you very much Amazon Prime!)

I like to refer to Hebrews 11 as the "faith" chapter of the Bible. This is one of my favorite places to look when I feel like my faith needs a refreshing and to be filled with hope:

> *Faith shows the reality of what we hope for;*
> *it is the evidence of things we cannot see.*
> *Hebrews 11:1*

Faith not only gets God's attention, but it reveals where our trust lies. In verse six we are able to capture the depth of what our faith does when it says:

It is impossible to please God without faith.
Anyone who wants to come to him must believe
that God exists and that he rewards
those who sincerely seek him.
Hebrews 11:6

Wow! Did you grasp it?! **It is impossible to please God without faith**. When we live, exist, and pray in faith, we live lives which are *pleasing* to God. Our trust in the Father pleases Him. Can you imagine a relationship without trust? I hope not. A relationship without trust isn't a relationship at all. The very foundation of a healthy connection to another person is being able to trust them! And when we live lives in faith, pleasing to God, then we live in a way which allows God to move the mountains in our paths which are keeping us from pressing forward toward what awaits us. Trust also gives God permission to access every part of our hearts, including how we perceive the world around us. Attempting to have a relationship with God without trust holds us back like prisoners, instead of the freedom to move forward in our purpose like our Father desires us to be.

As we persist to ask, seek, and knock, continually communing in prayer, it leads to a deep trust in God because these beautiful actions fan the flame of our purpose! They stoke the embers that contain those prayers we've prayed but haven't seen fulfilled yet. They blow on the smoke that swirls around our heart threatening to snuff out big dreams. They set ablaze the courage to believe no matter what life may look like. Deep trust in Jesus is a fire no raging storm can extinguish!

UNEARTHING THE HEART

Letting people get close used to be very difficult for me. I've always been a friend to any stranger, but getting vulnerable with people was a whole other experience I didn't allow myself to have. Hurt was like the elephant in the room of my life that I was used to ignoring. Abandonment wounds from childhood don't just go away, no matter how much you pretend they don't exist. And so when I began writing this book, I arrived at a place in my life when I realized I had a few weeds hanging around the garden of my heart. These unaddressed areas were keeping me from reaching my full potential. I may have surrendered the visible issues of my life, almost like clipping off the dandelion top of a destructive weed. But deep down, there were roots hidden below the surface of my heart beginning to affect my growth. If I didn't allow God to pull those things up by the root, I couldn't fully step into my destiny. I wouldn't have what I needed to press forward because it would have all been choked out by the weeds I allowed to fester in my heart.

When we "ask, seek, and knock," we make room for God to not only give us what we ask for in faith, but we also allow Him to strip off the things from our lives which don't belong there. I have learned from experience, one of the hardest things to walk through is this unearthing-excavation-type process of our heart. We really find out what we are willing to let go of when the Holy Spirit begins to reveal areas of our hearts which need to be dug up and burned like weeds. It is easy to allow God to burn up things we don't care for in our lives. People who hurt us. Situations which affect us negatively. These are all like bad weeds, sucking the life out of us. But how about those areas we have become familiar with? Those areas we don't think are too bad, but God desires to remove from us?

Occasionally without even realizing, we can allow roots to hang around. They aren't always obvious sins, but perhaps areas which keep us from moving forward. The music we listen to, the shows we watch on television, the conversations we take the time to partake in. Often times, these areas begin to affect the way we perceive the world around us. These things become what affects the way we see God!

Take a moment and think of some of the habits you have picked up over the years. Without placing these things on some sort of scale of good, bad, or worse, evaluate whether they are pleasing to God or not. When you think of the conversations you have, are they primarily negative? When you evaluate your thoughts, does insecurity seem to be your focus? It isn't as easy or comfortable to gauge those areas, but it is necessary to achieve true growth. Recently, through time in honest prayer, God revealed I had some messy areas--areas which were keeping me from fully running my race—that I needed to surrender to Him. When we process life with God through prayer regularly—evaluating what we are allowing to influence us—we can maintain the garden of our hearts and remove pesky weeds before they develop damaging roots.

When God desires to do a "new thing" in us, it seems to come when and in the form we least expect it. For me, this happened with someone I hold dear, my publisher. Our relationship is unique. She is both my publisher and close friend. Our relationship is like "iron sharpens iron" times 100! We have the ability to talk about the progress of my book and shopping in one conversation. One aspect of our relationship as publisher and author is coaching calls. This particular coaching session, she was asking how I was doing both spiritually, as well as professionally (I was in the process of writing this very book). While we were addressing how I was doing spiritually, she asked if there were areas in my life I was struggling in. I am not quite sure why, but I froze for a moment. Honestly, this was one of the hardest questions I have ever had to answer! It was as if time stood still and all the air in the room was sucked out! Ever have the feeling, similar to being on a stage in a filled auditorium and everyone is waiting for you to answer a life or death question? Well, this was one of those moments. Truth is, I didn't particularly care to talk about my faults. I was great at encouraging and pouring into others, but talking about my own struggles was rare! I realized I needed to let down my wall of pride and allow the Holy Spirit to really penetrate those undesirable roots. I had to give God room to do in my heart what was needed so I could continue in what He was calling me to. In this case, it was this very book I needed to finish. The results? God revealed I had deep roots to things I experienced over many years. Things I *thought* I let go of, prayed away, and discarded, but in reality, were still deeply rooted in my heart, affecting the way I perceived situations as well as people.

When we allow ourselves to be transparent, we reveal a true trust in God and allow Him to transform our hearts to look more and more like Jesus. There might be things in our hearts which shouldn't be there, preventing us from perceiving life as God has called us to see it through His eyes. It is the transformative process of submission to God which opens our hearts for the continual restoration we need for daily living in Him. It is a daily walk to live in submission! Presenting our bodies as a living sacrifice isn't about religious practices but rather a humble act inviting God to be an active part of every area of our lives, including the messy and unpleasant things. Transformation is an ongoing process where we acknowledge God knows what we need and don't need in our lives. Sometimes, He will use a close friend, pastor, or trusted leader to walk this journey of transparency with us. It is a beautiful choice to enter into intimacy with the One who knows what is best for us:

I appeal to you therefore, brothers, by the mercies of God, to present your bodies as a living sacrifice, holy and acceptable to God, which is your spiritual worship.
Romans 12:1 ESV

If we desire to live lives which truly represent Christ, then we have to surrender our whole self. In this process, we draw closer to the One who loves us most. As living sacrifices who are holy, we are acceptable to God. And in this position, we live in true worship to our Father. Worship has never been about a slow song at church or music we hear on the radio. Worship has always been about full submission to our God. It is our living sacrifice. Sacrificing our lives daily looks like giving God access to our hearts and permission to remove whatever is needed. When we do this, we are molded into His likeness and positioned to step into destiny.

When we fully submit, we trust that God is who He says He is. We can be confident when we pray according to the very words He implanted in the hearts of the men who wrote the Bible. We don't have to second guess if He will change His mind on us or walk away when we pray desperate prayers. We don't have to worry anxious thoughts of Him abandoning us if we doubt His timing or when we hold back our prayers in fear. Therefore, the same God who hears our hearts is the same one who sent His Son to the cross for our old wounds. Our identity is secure because He is secure! Our identity in Christ does not change because He does not change. And because of that security, we can trust that when we begin to lose our spark, His Holy Spirit is present within us to light us once more for His kingdom.

3

ANTICIPATE GOD-INTERRUPTIONS

An ideal Monday morning in our home looks like this: Get up at 5:30 a.m. to spend quiet time with God for thirty minutes. At 6:00, sign papers and get our daughter out the door to her middle school bus. At 6:30, our elementary school boys wake up, get ready, and get to their bus on time. At 7:15, I let out our two dogs, feed them, and sit down for a cup of tea. At 7:30, our oldest heads out the door for the high school bus. By 8:00, I let the dogs out again, then sit down for breakfast. As I said, this is my ideal, everything-goes-as-planned Monday morning. If only every Monday went off without a hitch like I just described. Sigh!

Interruptions to our well mapped out plan can be one of the most frustrating things to handle. During some seasons of my life, I have felt like there was a rise in these "life break-ins" where I'm certain I experienced a higher volume of interruptions. These times can leave anyone feeling like things still haven't changed, even after spending time in prayer and in the Word. At least, it can "seem" this way! But if we each take a step back and glance at it from a different perspective, is it possible that maybe, just maybe, God had been trying to get our attention?

In periods of increased stress and frustration, I've learned Scripture can be a great comfort to restore me through those rollercoaster times. It's renewing and purifying power is a gift to the Body of Christ:

> **To make her holy and clean, washed by the**
> **cleansing of God's word.**
> **Ephesians 5:26**

The gift of God's word is so much more than a "get out of jail free card" for our mind's troubles. Its transformative power assists us to not perceive our interruptions as problematic but rather an attention-getter from our Father in heaven. The word makes us holy and clean and keeps us this way as we remain steadfast in it. The Word of God is Christ Himself:

> **In the beginning the Word already existed.**
> **The Word was with God, and the Word was God.**
> **He existed in the beginning with God. God**
> **created everything through Him, and**
> **nothing was created except through Him.**
> **John 1:1-3**

As the scripture says, the Word was God and the Word became flesh (this is referring to Jesus when he stepped into the world in human form), and this is important to remember because it was Jesus who has made us holy and clean by His blood. Knowing and applying this to our everyday lives should change the way we handle everyday interruptions. Because Christ has made us holy, we should react in a holy (set apart, different) way, not like the world does, but with grace and patience.

So, how can we apply this to the way that we perceive all things? As children of God, because we have the Holy Spirit residing on the inside of us, we are called to view the most mundane to the most painful of interruptions as opportunities to get that much closer to the heart of Jesus. I have learned that when I face things I hadn't planned on, it will take a heart-to-heart with the God of the universe to walk through something I couldn't see coming. Even more, an interruption is another perfect God-moment to get a good peek at what the foundation of our lives is rooted in.

OUR PERCEPTION MATTERS

Our perception in this life will always determine our outcome. Interruptions are not different. They can be a consistent canceling of plans, a delay, or the inability to complete certain life goals. They often feel inconvenient and unfair. Yet, however interruptions may look, they are still—and will always be—an opportunity to sit at the feet of Jesus and simply be in His presence. I have learned from experience when I pause in the midst of my interruptions, I have the ability to see God moving right in the middle of it all.

When God planted the seed for the message of this book within my heart, I was interrupted beyond what I had ever experienced. For months, I had a nagging chronic pain which nearly consumed me. I had seen many specialists, only to have the pain intensify past the point of tears. From time to time, I felt so sorrowful and distant, as if I could not bring myself to find a Bible verse to soothe the pain. I know for a fact there is no lack of Scripture which could speak into my situation! But often, I would feel so foggy from several medications and utterly frazzled from the ongoing pain, and my mind could not grasp what it was I needed to do. I share my story, not to offer an invitation to a pity party, but to draw your attention to something God revealed to me in the middle of what I had been enduring: *Interruptions are an opportunity for Him to draw us near.*

As God drew me near by the power of His Spirit, He brought peace in a time I needed it most. During one day in particular in this same season of pain, God showed me a vision like I have never seen:

There I was, walking through a still stream. There were stones ranging in size all around me. Some were small rough river stones. Others were large and mossy, as well as some which were smooth from the constant running of water of the stream flowing quickly over them. The sand beneath those stones touched my feet and sent cold shivers down my spine as each toe made contact. As I stepped further into the stream, the water began to move. It began flowing so quickly over my feet, for a moment, I worried how I would cross this stream safely. Then, in an instant, I found myself walking through a meadow of sparkling green grass. The flowing river water had gone, and the flowing green blades were in its place. The green meadow was so tall, I didn't have to bend down to touch it! The blowing wind gave me peace which the raging stream did not. And in this still moment of the waving blades of grass in the valley, I heard the Lord whisper, "Exchange your storm for my peace." Right in this very moment, the Holy Spirit revealed I had a choice. Would I continue viewing my situation as a major "interruption" or begin to offer up my storm as a sacrifice in exchange for the peace He promised me?

You see, God does not cause our pain. But He does *use* our experience of pain to draw us closer (neither does He bring about the struggle and torment we face in this life). As He draws us near, he offers us the opportunity to come sit at His feet, even when we're in the midst of whatever it is we may be facing. Because it is there where our perspective is no longer focused on the trial that we see in front of us, but the Christ Who bears all burdens and lives within us. The Apostle Paul is a perfect Biblical example of someone who experienced some of the greatest torment on this earth. But, it was his full submission to the Father which led him to understand our weaknesses are not our shame but an opportunity.

In every struggle, Christ is revealed:

> *My grace is always more than enough for you,*
> *and my power finds its full expression*
> *through your weakness.*
> *2 Corinthians 12:9a TPT*

His Grace always meets us in our weaknesses. No matter how weak we may feel, it will always lead to a chance for God to show us His power in the middle of it. And so our interruptions are an opportunity for us to step into the supernatural and let Christ shine through us.

REJOICE IN TRIALS

I absolutely hate pain! It was never meant to be the path we were ever supposed to take. The pain that I have felt in my body for the past two years has led me into some dark places. I have felt feelings of emptiness and depression. I have questioned whether I would ever feel "normal" again or if I would be able to be who I was before all of this. I have even wondered how God could allow me to experience such a feeling. When you are in the middle of the fight of your life, one that threatens to snuff out the faith that burns in your heart, you think some really low thoughts. I wish as a Christian I didn't have to endure pain or go through tough times! I wish that when we accept Christ, we could just live lives full of butterfly and rainbows. But that isn't the world we live in. It is filled with sickness, pain, death. But, it is in those dark places that Jesus reaches out His hand to show us how to view our circumstances through the eyes of the Father. Some storms in our life go instantaneously, some go eventually, and some never do. But when we capture the view of the Father, we are captivated by what He is doing in the storm instead of the storm itself. The Apostle Paul captured this view. And like me, he too faced a lot of earthly pain.

I reference Paul significantly more than others because he knew trials as much as he knew the cause he was created for. He understood we could endure through the most difficult of trials which come our way because of the confident hope found in Christ:

*We can rejoice, too, when we run into problems
and trials, for we know that they help us
develop endurance. And endurance develops
strength of character, and character strengthens
our confident hope of salvation. And this hope
will not lead to disappointment. For we know
how dearly God loves us, because he has given
us the Holy Spirit to fill our hearts with his love.
Romans 5:3-5*

Paul was a poster boy for finding joy even when carrying burdens. In this letter to the Romans, he was illustrating to the church that every single trial a believer will face offers an opportunity to develop endurance. He was well acquainted with difficult experiences as well as the strength of character that is developed in the process. He was familiar with the rising of the waves of life, yet he remained rooted and confident in who God is and His love for us!

When my pain began, I had no idea of what God would develop in me. I couldn't see past what was happening to me! It has taken time and patience to evaluate my perspective. But in the process, as I began to trust that the Father really had me by the hand, joy began to fill me. Growth began to take place as God was pruning away my old perception of who He is in my sunshine, as well as who He is in my storm. For the first time in my life, it was in facing the greatest trials of my life where I had allowed myself to be stretched beyond my previous capacity. And what I discovered when my stormy seas did not calm, was that my perception of God and trials were not firmly rooted in Him and His word. I am thankful that He uses those storms to dig our roots down deep in our trust in Him. I believe this is what Paul was teaching the church. That we can believe in God's goodness and trust the growth process, even though it hurts.

It is an innate human characteristic to grapple and try to make sense of things in life when we would rather they disappear. But it is Paul who reminds us of the importance of enduring trials no matter what they are. In the middle of the hardest seasons, God uses whatever we give Him permission to use in order to strengthen and grow our faith:

> *For the sake of Christ, then, I am content*
> *with weaknesses, insults, hardships,*
> *persecutions, and calamities. For*
> *when I am weak, then I am strong.*
> *2 Corinthians 12:10 ESV*

Paul understood, because of the Holy Spirit within us, we can rejoice and endure our trials as well as remain content in them knowing God's strength is sufficient when we are weak in our suffering. So, when the mountains we have prayed to leave don't move, and the storms we faithfully pray against remain, we can choose to believe these trials are faith builders. We can remember God is with us and has given us the ability to see each situation, good and difficult, with His eyes and face it with His strength.

CHOOSE GOD'S PERSPECTIVE

In the midst of both the enjoyable and hard times, rejoicing will always be our best choice. Why? Because our Father in Heaven loves us so much. He has given us free will to do so. Is it our normal reaction to shout for joy when we're going through difficulties? No! This is why the presence of the Holy Spirit is so significant. We won't naturally rejoice and remain content, but if we turn to the

God who is inside of us and lean on His power, we can access a supernatural joy and peace even in the middle of a raging sea. When we decide to find something to rejoice about no matter what the circumstances, we are choosing God's will for our lives. We can serve and worship God in the way we respond to all situations. As Christians, we have chosen a life in relationship with Him. And each day, we get to decide who will we serve with our actions (ourselves or our God).   •

God loves us and desires us to fulfill all He created us for. But, if I am being honest, sometimes it doesn't always feel like He loves me, especially when I am faced with difficult interruptions like death and sickness. In times where we don't understand His love, we must learn to switch from what we *feel* to what we *know* is the truth: He **DOES** love us. He loves us so much. He allows things like interruptions to draw us to the throne where we have the freedom to lay down every single hurt. In His presence, like a good Father, we can rest in the peace He promises, shift our perspective, and exchange sorrow and emptiness for the overwhelming joy He gives which fills us with strength (Nehemiah 8:10).

Choosing a new perspective in our struggle is never easy, but it is worth it! Truthfully, it may not feel like a choice when you are overwhelmed with things beyond your control. Nevertheless, we always have a choice. The choice will, however, require something of us. A sacrifice of self; sacrifice of the desire to control each and every area of our lives. We have the choice to accept the opportunity to lay down what holds us hostage and keeps us from peace.

During the hard season when I experienced severe and unexplained pain, I cried out to God daily. Every waking minute was filled with brokenness. All I was confident and secure in felt far away. I felt like I was in a clear, soundproof box--trapped in my own mind. Everyone around me could see me and speak to me, but they could not hear the screams of my soul. My mind felt imprisoned by the medicine to keep my pain controlled. And day after day, I pleaded to God. Like King David, I felt so isolated, and it seemed God was distant from me. Many moments were filled with anguish as I prayed honestly to my Father:

Why, O Lord, do you stand far away?
Why do you hide yourself in times of trouble?
Psalm 10:1

In those moments of loneliness, honesty, and brokenness, God was there right in the middle of my torment. But I had to give Him permission to interrupt my life. It was then that I came to understand He was not asking me to "accept" my trial but rather see it from His perspective. I allowed Him to reveal His purpose in each and every struggle. As I opened my heart, He revealed my pain was not from Him, however, He would use it for my good:

For I know the thoughts that I think toward you,
says the Lord, thoughts of peace and not of evil,
to give you a future and a hope.
Jeremiah 29:11 NKJV

I chose Him above my pain. I chose His perspective. I chose to trust God at His word. I chose to believe what He allows me to go through (even the hard things) are to give me "a future and a hope." And what does this future and hope look like? It is what Paul spoke of in Romans 5:5, no matter what we face, "...we know how dearly God loves us."

We need to reflect on this the next time we face something beyond our limits. Will we give God permission to interrupt our lives? Will we be willing to look at difficulties as a way He will be glorified through us? Not everyone in our lives will understand. Not everyone will even agree. People might tell us to speak to our mountains and calm our storms. Those prayers are genuine and necessary, and we must be able to discern when it is time for those prayers and when it is time to pray thanksgiving and stand upon His grace.

I want to make my point clear. A relationship with God is not a magic potion to poof away hard times. Rather it is a relationship which defines our identity and how we perceive the world around us.

The Word reminds us we can still trust God when things don't go as planned. We can still believe He is faithful even if the prayer we've been praying doesn't come to pass in the way we expected. We can still serve Him faithfully when the healing, or the finances, or the unsaved family member doesn't change within the time frame we hoped for.

God knows what we are going through at all times. He has not left or become suddenly uninterested in our struggle. Rather, He is ever-present at the place we can often delay going to: the altar. As we walk in our destiny, we will always face trials and interruptions. But as we pursue Him, our interruptions change from inconveniences to opportunities to be in the presence of the Almighty God. And in this place of intimacy, He will be waiting to spend time with us and walk with us through the valley:

> *We are pressed on every side by troubles, but we are not crushed. We are perplexed, but not driven to despair. We are hunted down, but never abandoned by God. We get knocked down, but we are not destroyed. Through suffering, our bodies continue to share in the death of Jesus so that the life of Jesus may also be seen in our bodies.*
> *2 Corinthians 4:8-10*

Before we end this chapter, I would like you to join me in a declaration. I believe if we have the truth of God's word to hold tight to when our world is shaken, we can depend on His word to settle our unsteady ground. Because of the indwelling of the Holy Spirit, it is possible to remain firm through any and everything. We are people who have the grace to look at disruptions as opportunities to draw close to God and see our every situation through His eyes. We don't become less His when we become unsteady or when we ask why. We don't scare God away with our wishes for the storm to end. We are secure in Him! We can look at disruptions with a new perspective and keep the flame of faith glowing brightly in our lives as a believer, as opposed to allowing our difficulties to dim our light:

I choose God's perspective. I choose to walk on the waves of each and every storm which may come my way. I choose to pursue His presence, not for what He can do for me but for who He is to me. Come hell or high water, I will keep my eye on the One who is my salvation. As His child, I know I can pray boldly for my storm to end, and I can stand courageously by faith even if it doesn't change in my timing. So, I will continue to stand in faith to endure all things, as well as the discernment of how to navigate them. Interruptions are always opportunities to grow deeper in Him.

PART TWO

When we know who we are and to WHOM we belong, we'll be intentional about accomplishing the great mission before us. God's heart is for people to find freedom. Therefore, our mission will be the same. This is who we are as the body of Jesus Christ. In this part of the book, we will learn to stir the flames which have dimmed or possibly have burned out and learn to live on fire for the Kingdom of our God.

4

PIERCE THE SILENCE

The hardest part of stepping into our destiny is taking the first step. Often, we keep a list (intentionally or unintentionally) of all the things keeping us from starting. Some things in life may have truly delayed us, like interruptions. At other times, we are what stops us from moving forward. Burnout, control issues, lack of confidence, and even sin are just some of the things plaguing us and keeping us from remaining on task. We may find ourselves focused on those things which are contrary to who we were called to be:

> *I want to do what is good, but I don't.*
> *I don't want to do what is wrong, but I do it anyway.*
> **Romans 7:19**

However, the Bible does not list these as approved justifications for the fire in our soul to grow dim! We are not under the power of sin. We are children of the living God. We were set free from the things in this life which can steal our focus from the journey:

For the law of the Spirit of life in Christ Jesus
has made me free from the law of sin and death.
Romans 8:2 NKJV

The Spirit of life in Christ Jesus defeated every single thing that threatens to slow us down in life (or stop us all together) at the cross. From those things that seem like small hindrances, like a pebble in our shoes when we walk, to those that block us like boulders. He overcame all things that stand in the way of the treasure hidden in us and the destiny laid out before us! So, as we begin to grasp the weight of moving forward in our purpose, we must first come face to face with why the cost is so great to remain on fire.

Jesus was intentional in all He did and accomplished. Every single miracle, encounter, and teaching was done to glorify the Father. Glorifying the Father can never be half-hearted. I believe it can never be done beautifully with partially committed intentions. Just as running a race without shoes would be difficult and limit a runner's mission, we as children of God should not expect to eliminate the darkness if our own flames are poorly lit. This world is crying out for light, and so we must stoke the fires of Heaven in our souls to shine bright!

You are the light of the world. A city that is set
on a hill cannot be hidden. Nor do they light a
lamp and put it under a basket, but on a
lampstand, and it gives light to all who are
in the house. Let your light so shine before
men, that they may see your good
works and glorify your Father in heaven.
Matthew 5:14-16 NKJV

If we allow our hearts to burn bright, we will find that the world is looking to see if the God we speak of is faithful when our world turns upside down. People always watch to see if we remain secure when nothing seems to go our way. They want to know: Is it possible for a person to have peace, stand secure, and not crumble when you are in a storm? These onlookers take notice and will watch and try to understand why we believe what we believe. Why? Because they are also searching.

You see, our journey isn't just about us! This race of life is meant to "glorify your Father in heaven"! We have a very real enemy who desires to snuff out the fire in our souls for this very reason. He doesn't want us to have an impact and help other people overcome problems and interruptions. Satan will consistently whisper his lies into our souls because he wants us to forget WHO we have inside of us. He even has a way of speaking through others to keep us from remembering that we have the power of the living God within us! He desires us to overlook that our promised companion would remain with us at all times. Jesus told His disciples when He ascended, He would send someone in His place. He wanted them (and all His followers) to know He was not going to leave them alone to walk this life, but they would have this person indwelling within them to be there every step of the way:

> *Nevertheless, I tell you the truth.*
> *It is to your advantage that I go away;*
> *for if I do not go away, the Helper*
> *will not come to you; but if I*
> *depart, I will send Him to you.*
> *John 16:7 NKJV*

The Holy Spirit was a promise given to us so that we could be able to fully walk through this life. We were never meant to barely make it or struggle through everything that comes our way. As He counsels us, encourages us, directs us, and fulfills His role in our lives as believers, He keeps us ablaze with the purpose for the expansion of God's Kingdom right here on earth. And this is what I believe Jesus' life revealed to us; Relationship.

I believe there are quite a few twisted doctrines today which attempt to remove or misconstrue a very valid and Biblical truth: Jesus was fully God and fully man (as if He needed to choose one status to have a relationship with the Father). Even though He was fully divine, He obediently walked the earth as one of us, and He came to know first-hand what it would cost to serve God completely. The Bible reveals story after story of Jesus' personal experience with the struggles we humans face. He was persecuted, accused wrongly of crimes, laughed at, and the list goes on. Yet, because of His relationship with the Father, He overcame every single one:

> *Now that we know what we have—Jesus, this great*
> *High Priest with ready access to God—let's not let it*
> *slip through our fingers. We don't have a priest*
> *who is out of touch with our reality. He's been*
> *through weakness and testing, experienced it*
> *all—all but the sin. So let's walk right up to*
> *him and get what he is so ready to give.*
> *Take the mercy, accept the help.*
> *Hebrews 4:14-16 MSG*

Before He laid the foundation of the heavens and the earth, God was fully aware that some days, weeks, and even years would feel too overbearing for us. I believe He foreknew there would be times when our greatest fight of faith would not be against an external enemy, but instead, within ourselves.

God knew there would be times where our greatest enemy would be the seeds we allowed to take root within our own hearts. The seeds would eventually become full-grown weeds of damaging lies about our identity which cause us to forget who we are in Him. Like thorns, those words cut us deep as we replayed painful memories over and over in our minds. These hurtful statements can eventually grow deep roots within our hearts-- and these often hidden roots secretly snuff out our fiery flame, once lit ablaze by our salvation.

I have experienced the wounds left behind from past words and memories. And, when left unaddressed, these hurts grew deep roots within the garden of my heart. They seemed to remain dormant for a season, but subtly they began affecting every part of life, similar to a wrapping vine which covers the most beautiful old homes. At one time, they were the jewels of the neighborhood. But unkempt and unseen, they became dark, hidden, and unclaimed.

We must allow the Holy Spirit to continually speak over all these areas within us. It is He who heals those sore and broken places hidden deep within. As children of God, our inheritance is "healing" not "hurting." These wounds of untruthful words and painful memories have been defeated and overcome by Jesus at the cross (John 16:33), and now, we have to walk out the application with His Spirit.

When Jesus ascended back to Heaven, He sent us the Holy Spirit as a gift to be a comforter to those in the family of God. He is the gift who whispers truth to our soul. He reminds us, we are enough, qualified, and HIS! But while the Holy Spirit is always present, often we can forget about Him. I know I have.

At times, we can revert to the familiarity of those weeds and deep thorny roots over the unknown of what He offers because we are afraid. Perhaps we fear if He ever got close enough, He would see the cracks in our façade! Sometimes we worry He would find out we don't have it all together. (Side note: Reality check. He already knows! Ha! And, He chose us anyway.) And this is just it, the Holy Spirit is the gift who heals all those shattered pieces of ourselves and calms every anxiety. But, we have to be courageous enough to let it all go. He's kind and good, and won't take anything from us we don't willingly and bravely bring out into the open and lay at His feet.

The Holy Spirit does not have a loud, barking voice echoing with cynicism and anger wrestling us into peace. No! He is peace! He is our comforter! He is the Spirit of the living God offering us clear vision and insight in this life when things seem bleak. He extends all of the peace we need, which surpasses anything we could ever understand (Philippians 4:7), but we must invite Him to do so.

In some seasons, living our lives for the glory of God's Kingdom may seem impossible. Occasionally, it may feel unimaginable to even accept the peace of the Holy Spirit needed to take the journey. And this feeling is warranted. We were NEVER meant to walk this kingdom-living path on our own. Actually, it is IMPOSSIBLE to do it by ourselves. But having consistent peace and powerfully walking out our kingdom mandate isn't impossible with God:

> ### *For nothing will be impossible with God.*
> ### *Luke 1:37 NASB*

When we are able to grasp the depths of God's grace--believing our Heavenly Father is always there to help us-- and realize we are not silent orphaned bystanders trapped outside His Kingdom walls, we begin to live as Kingdom citizens. We can confidently walk as children, inheritors, and carriers of the Kingdom of Almighty God, as we sync heaven and earth. God has called us all to bring His Kingdom to this earth, and the first step in walking this out is believing God is with you. Let him constantly reveal weeds that have planted themselves in your heart and seek continual healing from lies and hurts. As we seek His peace throughout the journey and remember the Holy Spirit is there to empower us, we can boldly begin walking out our calling.

WALK IN GRACE

The society we live in is filled with desire. Anything can be purchased. In fact, money is no issue. Or so it seems. Using credit is always an option--buy now, pay later!

When I was in my freshman year of college, I was 17 and away from home for the first time. My past history with money wasn't the greatest. My depth in budgeting was earn it, then spend it. So imagine the ideas I had when I was told that I qualified for a credit card. All I saw were dollar signs! That was the beginning of irresponsible money management. One credit card turned in three. And if I wanted something and I didn't have the cash for it, I used my credit cards. Boy, was I wrong! Those cards were used up and defaulted on quick. When my husband and I got married and started having children, those old debts began to follow me. It took maturity, prayer, and our savings to turn our money situation right-side-up. That experience taught us both how to properly steward our finances and credit. Regrettably, this isn't always the outcome for everyone.

Financing is freely available to anyone who will sign an agreement with the hopes of getting whatever their heart desires. The hidden and frightening reality is the willingness to sign a debt for the sake of a want can be a dangerous game. Borrowing with the intention of paying off the debt should be our goal. To borrow without considering a budget, or with limited intention to pay it off, isn't the best choice for our finances. Unfortunately, this is how many of us lived before we understood Christ has paid our debt. We may have believed we needed to repay our own debt of sin, but God has a different way:

> *For by grace you have been saved through faith,*
> *and that not of yourselves; it is the gift of God,*
> *not of works, lest anyone should boast.*
> *Ephesians 2:8-9 NKJV*

Biblically, living like we are working off debt is contrary to what God has always envisioned for His people. Salvation has never been something which could be financed or even paid off by one's own sheer will or works:

> *I become righteous through faith in Christ.*
> *For God's way of making us right with*
> *Himself depends on faith.*
> *Philippians 3:9b*

What does financing have anything to do with righteousness or grace? When we come to comprehend the way God has established His Kingdom, then we will begin to understand, like any earthly kingdom, God's Kingdom also has an economy. I want to define financing to connect the pieces together.

Financing is defined by Merriam Webster's Dictionary as:

> **"the act or process or an instance of raising or**
> **providing funds."**[4]

Let's plunge below the surface of this definition so we can grasp the powerful truth of a Kingdom mindset, and how God's economy affects us.

There are two main types of financing we are familiar within the banking system: debt and equity. Debt, as most individuals know, must be paid back to the lender. In order to mortgage a home or finance a car, we usually borrow from a bank. As responsible borrowers, we then return what we borrow in the form of monthly payments. Until the money we borrow is paid as agreed, it is considered a debt.

Equity, on the other hand, does not need to be paid back. It is the money value of a property we gain as borrowers. As we are slowly paying off our debt for a home or car, we are building up equity which does not need to be returned to the bank but is ours to keep. What was once the banks is now ours. Ownership rights have been transferred from the financer to the one financing. The title is now signed over with full rights to the one who paid it off. Now, let's apply this to a spiritual concept such as God's Kingdom.

At one time, we were separated from God. Before we accepted the sacrifice Jesus made and we received salvation by faith, we owed a great debt to God: a sacrifice to cover our sin! But through Christ, all of this changed:

> *But now you have been united with Christ Jesus.*
> *Once you were far away from God,*
> *but now you have been brought near to him*
> *through the blood of Christ.*
> *Ephesians 2:13*

As children of God, Christ paid our debt. When we were in sin, at a great cost, we financed all the desires of our flesh in order to please our flesh. But through Christ's death and resurrection, His sacrifice paid ALL of our debt ONCE AND FOR ALL as we read in Romans 5.

We could never pay the debt back for our sin! NEVER! But God did not ask us to. Rather, the only thing we give is our hearts. Not for payment but as a covenant. As we accept the price paid for us, by faith, we are made righteous in God's sight. This is God's economy:

> *God saved you by his grace when you*
> *believed. And you can't take credit for this;*
> *it is a gift from God. Salvation is not*
> *a reward for the good things we have done,*
> *so none of us can boast about it.*
> *For we are God's masterpiece. He has*

created us anew in Christ Jesus,
so we can do the good things he
planned for us long ago.
Ephesians 2:8-10

We have covered the truth that Christ paid our debt in full. But what of our equity? As I covered earlier, equity is unlike debt. It does not need to be paid back. Rather it surrenders ownership rights to the one who paid the debt in full. Who then holds the title? Our Almighty God! Jesus' blood paid off our debt, therefore Father God holds the title. To what? To our fully surrendered lives! As it says in Ephesians 2:10, "We are God's masterpiece."

Our days of leading our lives of sin are in the past. We are new creations in Christ Jesus (2 Corinthians 5:17)! We have surrendered our hearts over completely to Christ. And because of this, we are no longer our own, but we are one with Christ (1 Corinthians 6:17). As part of God's Kingdom, we don't have to live hindered by our past. The past is behind us. The old has fallen away. We do not have to accept the garments of past mistakes to be placed on us and keep us from moving forward in our destiny. Jesus Christ has paid for our sin. We are in covenant and live in everlasting fellowship because of Jesus. We are free to fully shine in the purpose God has planned for our lives.

RECOGNIZE YOUR POSITION

A child of God who truly recognizes their position within the Kingdom of God will be more effective than one who does not. Let me be clear, the act of *being effective* is not to be associated with the act of *more works* but rather an understanding of one's purpose. Sometimes we can get so busy doing works, we miss out on why we do what we do.

As parents, my husband and I get to love our children and watch them grow. Part of that growing they experience is living a life that reflects who they are as part of our family and the family of God. Our youngest child is the one who has come to experience this the most. He is wild and free which means we have to discuss boundaries and self-control quite often. Don't get me wrong, every one of our kids has to be reminded; he just needs it a bit more than the others. So, from time to time, he comes home upset because he received correction at school for his behavior. When he comes running through the front door after school with "the face," we know it has been one of *those* days.

One day in particular, he came home in tears because it was treasure box day and he didn't get to pick a treasure. His behavior chart showed that he hadn't earned a treasure based on his behavior that week. He was furious. He said, "I am sorry, and I won't do it again." Based on the classroom rules, he would get another chance next week. But, according to him, that still was not a fair deal!

After his snack (and some relax time), we got a chance to sit and chat about what happened. I asked him, "Who are you?" He thought it was silly, but he indulged me, "I am a son of God." I sure didn't expect this from my rambunctious 7-year-old, but I continued on, "How does God say we should behave?" He grunted and mumbled, "With self-control." I smiled and said, "What about as a Tubbs kid?" He smiled, "With good character and helpfulness." I could tell he had been listening! "That's right," I said. We finished our chat with reminders that good character and self-control show our world who we are in God's family. It invites other people to get a peek at who Jesus is, but when we misbehave or lose control, we don't get to do that. We behave on purpose because we love God not just for treasures. Treasures are fun, but they can't be why we show who we are. Jesus has to be why. Surprisingly enough, he sat still long enough to hear me finish. We exchanged an eskimo kiss (rubbing our noses together), and he ran off to play.

My book *In Pursuit of Purpose* covers the concept of being intentional. By nature, intentionality creates a dividing line between the act of *living on purpose* and simply *going through the motions*. As children of God, through an intentional relationship with Him, we have learned we were created—not only on purpose—but for a purpose (Genesis 1:27-28). We were placed on this earth to be wise stewards of creation. Jesus evidenced this well through His life on earth. Through His relationship with the Father, He developed and commissioned disciples to carry on the work of the Kingdom here on earth. Jesus then gave the mandate to all of us who would become His disciples:

> **Therefore, go and make disciples of all the**
> **nations, baptizing them in the name of the**
> **Father and the Son and the Holy Spirit.**
> **Teach these new disciples to obey**
> **all the commands I have given you.**
> **And be sure of this: I am with you always,**
> **even to the end of the age.**
> **Matthew 28:19-20**

When we intentionally live our lives as God created us to, we begin making disciples and start actively expanding the Kingdom of God. This is how we live effectively. Those who live intentionally in the Kingdom do so because they understand why they are doing it! On the contrary, those who fall into the trap of works in hopes of gaining a position, do so because they have not yet recognized who they are in the Kingdom. They don't know the position they already stand in. The enemy will trap us if we don't know who we are and where we stand--and often, He does this through a misunderstanding of Scripture.

I believe many of God's children have misunderstood their

position in God's Kingdom because of what they've been taught. Inadvertently, the concept of doing work to earn a position in the Kingdom has gone unchallenged and has led many to live as slaves of God rather than friends (James 2:22). It is that lack of revelation of relationship and right-standing through Jesus that leads us to miss this precious opportunity.

If we back up just a few verses before the verse above, we find one of the most quoted passages in Scripture. It is a reminder from James that I believe we could all use as believers:

Faith without works is <u>dead</u>.
James 2:20, NKJV, emphasis added

If you aren't sure of how God views you, it can be pretty easy to view this verse as the prescription for a works-filled salvation. From personal experience, I have chosen this path in my own walk with God. There were days I was so fixed on what I needed to do *for* God that I missed times to just sit *with* Him and hear Him do the talking. In seasons He wanted to just hold me, I spent reading the newest devotional. Mornings He wanted to hear me sing out praises as a sweet fragrance, I spent writing a blog. None of these were bad things! But on those days, they missed the whole point of being with Him. It must be like being invited to a friend's home for a wonderful time together, only for her to spend the whole evening in the kitchen slaving for me. When, in reality, I just came to be with her (that would be a bummer). Heard of the story of Mary and Martha?

Now as they went on their way, Jesus entered
a village. And a woman named Martha welcomed
him into her house. And she had a sister called Mary,
who sat at the Lord's feet and listened to his teaching.
But Martha was distracted with much serving.
And she went up to him and said, "Lord, do

you not care that my sister has left me to
serve alone? Tell her then to help me."
But the Lord answered her, "Martha, Martha,
you are anxious and troubled about many things,
but one thing is necessary. Mary has chosen the good
portion, which will not be taken away from her."
Luke 10:38-42

The very message of the Bible from beginning to end reveals God never intended us to work for Him. His plan for us has always been to be in relationship with Him, and from this connection, we'd inevitably reveal His glory. Like Mary in the story, this will always flow freely from our time spent in true relationship with Him.

As we move forward into the next chapter, I pray that anything that may have caused you to believe anything contrary to who God says you are to Him will fall away and that you are positioned to move forward in freedom and security, having no reservations about how God views you as His child. When we see ourselves as *friends* of God, we shine bright and confidently, walking out the mission we have been given.

5

ENGAGE THE MISSION AHEAD

I'll explain later in this chapter, but I want you to know from my own experience, I know firsthand what it is like to misunderstand who I am in Christ, and therefore have no real passion or fire to walk out my calling. But, when we fully recognize who we are in Christ, we will then understand there is a great mission to accomplish.

Facebook has this feature that reminds you of something you posted in the past. Those memories can bring you back to the very moment in time the picture was taken, pictures of your kids when they were small, vacations that your family loved, and the cute puppy pictures (all the squeals). But then there are those memories that you wish would disappear in a black hole. The ones of when you weren't always so "mature" in your walk with Christ. I despise Facebook on those days! They show me how self-righteous or judgemental I was in the past. About five years ago after a 3 year Facebook hiatus, I was ready to pull the plug or delete everything because I was ashamed at who I used to be. I didn't like that person at all! But the Holy Spirit stopped me and reminded me of something;

without security in Christ, our lives overflow with wounding words instead of life-giving ones. I am thankful for the Holy Spirit. He can take a moment of shame and quickly replace it with the truth: I am not who I used to be, and there is still so much growing ahead. Our past does not define us unless we let it.

When we fully recognize who we are in Christ, we then understand there is a great mission to accomplish. Not for our glory, but for God's. The reason why we push on and continue to stoke the fire of our calling is because people's very lives depend on it (like mine did). I had people around me who knew who they were in Christ which challenged me to seek God for who He created me to be! This is why we must discover who we are and all we are called to do. Our mission is people. Why? Because bringing freedom, love, and purpose to the hearts and lives of the people of the world is the mission of our Father in Heaven.

The mission to rescue people has *always* been God's idea. Restoration is not what He does selectively; it is who He is innately! Healing the broken-hearted; adopting the fatherless into His family. and forgiving what the world has considered unforgivable are the very core of His nature. He is the C.E.O. of deliverance. His plan was never to send Jesus just to reach a select group of individuals and ignore the rest, but to redeem the heart of every single person on the face of this earth. And *we*, those who He has liberated from sin and separation, get the privilege to partner with Him to reach those who have not yet been freed. We get to collaborate with the Creator of heaven and earth to be walking ambassadors of freedom to a world imprisoned in depravity.

It is disturbing to witness the many who are broken and hurting in this world. The world is looking for hope and is unable to find it. Satan has deceived them into believing there is no way out. He has misled them into settling for a fragmented existence. Don't get me wrong, there are very real consequences for choices we make which can lead us into difficult situations, but we always want to give true credit to who is behind every bit of it. If there is suffering, deception, division, and the like, we know exactly who receives the recognition: Satan himself (Ephesians 6:11). Here's an example.

It is like one of those days which begin wonderfully, then it suddenly seems to go downhill. And, instead of letting it go, a big grand cinema begins to play in our minds of all the things that could possibly go wrong. What starts as a molehill instantly becomes a mountain (in our mind), and even though everything began so great, it quickly turn into being the worst day of our life! Well, I'll be the first person to go ahead and raise my hand and admit: "Been there!" Wonder why that is? Why do our minds become the stage of scenarios we wouldn't want in our lives?

I once heard someone say, "We need to spend more time thinking about what we think about." In other words, we have to be like guardians of our thought life. So many things run through our minds so casually, so much so, that if we aren't mindful, we end up believing those wild movies on the screen of our minds. God created our minds to automatically filter thoughts. But, it is up to us to take stewardship over them. Either we will allow God's truth to remain or our enemy's lies. One will keep us rooted in Christ, while the other will steal our identity. What we allow to settle in our minds has more power than we might think. If our enemy can make us believe his lies are true, then we will live from this place. So it is most important that what we allow to stay will be God's truth that will ultimately guide our every decision. This is why the Bible reminds us:

We are human, but we don't wage war as humans do. We use God's mighty weapons, not worldly weapons, to knock down the strongholds of human reasoning and to destroy false arguments. We destroy every proud obstacle that keeps

people from knowing God.
We capture their rebellious thoughts
and teach them to obey Christ.
2 Corinthians 10:3-5

If we accept every single thought which enters our minds as truth, including Satan's sneaky lies, then the course of our lives will reveal the very same destruction. We must understand the nature of Satan is to masquerade. His talent: Pretending. He is the master of simulation. He goes about plotting ways to trick humanity into believing everything he displays as truth. We must remember that no matter what he may say, he is and will always be a liar. No matter what may *seem* true in any moment of time, these lies of the enemy are really a strategic plan to put out the fire in souls for the Kingdom cause. Scripture says:

Even Satan disguises himself as an angel of light.
2 Corinthians 11:14b

If he can keep us from recognizing truth through his many disguises, then he can keep us from fulfilling all which God has destined for His creation. Because of the enemy's lies, there are people hurting everywhere we look. Isaiah says we are the work of God's hands, and God is the Potter—you could think of Satan as the false potter (Isaiah 64:8). The Devil brings destruction into the world, and in his wake, people are left broken, similar to cracked and fragile vessels which are molded and painted over carelessly. Instead of feeling valued by a loving Father, they become numb, deprived of the knowledge of God's extravagant love for them!

The world (and even the church) is bursting with innumerable hurting souls who wear masks which proclaim they are doing just fine, when, in reality, they are afflicted souls—perhaps drowning in depression, self-loathing, or are emotionally crippled. These wounded hearts cry out to be seen, heard, and loved. *These* are whom Jesus went out of His way to reach. And to these whom the church of Jesus Christ is commissioned to reach every single day (Matthew 28:19).

We must never forget, at one time in our own lives, we were like these fragile vessels needing a potter to restore us. Many of us were like abandoned clay pots left out in the weather losing value and purpose. In the past, we were victims of our enemy, filled with despair, imprisoned in our sin and shame. But, Jesus Christ pursued our hearts and liberated us through His sacrifice (John 3:16). And now we are FREE! We are no longer broken and shattered; we are restored. We were once orphaned; we have now been adopted into the family of God. Where there was lack, we are now filled with purpose and value. Peter reminds us:

> *Once you were not a people, but now you are*
> *God's people; once you had not received mercy,*
> *but now you have received mercy.*
> *1 Peter 2:10 ESV*

There are many in the body of Christ who still believe the lies of the enemy and have not received this revelation of God's mercy in their own lives. They are still broken and still unsure of how precious they are to the Father. I have absolutely been in this position in my own life where I cried out to be heard. I grew up going to church, but I still felt so distant from God (He wasn't distant, but I didn't know this). I was completely unaware I lacked the most fundamental and essential aspect of Christianity: Relationship with Jesus. I was pretty sure Jesus Christ died for sin as far as knowledge was concerned, but I had no idea in my heart why He did or if His offer was rescinded when I didn't do or say all the right things. I wandered in search of something, someone, and anything to provide security and completion in place of what I was missing. I thought the only way to fill this void as a new believer was to go to church more often.

I found myself drifting back and forth between devoted churchgoer and overzealous religious person. Both sounded good on paper (I had these listed on my mental resume of things I believed made me worthy of acceptance by God). But, I thank the Lord He didn't allow me to settle in this false sense of righteousness. He would not permit me to stay in a place where my relationship was relegated to *what I did*. Instead, He drew me to His heart and revealed to my lonely heart *what Jesus did* at the cross.

One Sunday morning, 700 miles away from all I knew, God interrupted my whole doctrine of church. There, He shook loose all which I thought kept me safe. I thought I could hide my pain from people who didn't really know me. I wanted to fake like I had it all together. In many ways, this affected how I viewed my relationship with God. I didn't pray openly and honestly but rather in a formal way that avoided all intimacy. Thank God that He knows us so much better than we know ourselves! He invaded my heart with peace, love, and open arms. It was there where my true relationship with the Creator of the universe began. I traded my Sunday and holiday experience for an everyday love fest with my Heavenly Father, which would soon affect every person I encountered. My personal works of relationship became a life of faith. This is when I began understanding our true mission as the body of Christ, the church.

So, how is such a great mission supposed to look in our everyday lives? Are we supposed to quit our jobs and become missionaries to a foreign nation? Well, not unless God reveals this to us. The real question we should be asking ourselves every single day is: How are we to balance both this mission and our lives? Short answer: Relationship. Long answer: Relationship. Why? Because the God of mercy lives inside us.

Through mercy, God has revealed Himself to us (the church of Jesus Christ). And it is also through mercy God reveals Himself to the world (those who are yet to know Jesus Christ) through *us*.

What does God's mercy have to do with His mission for people? Through this same mercy, sin and shame which once ruled *our* lives have been defeated, and once-hurting people (like we were) are saved from the endless rut of sin which only serves but to isolate us from truth and freedom (Romans 10:13). And through this same mercy, the church has been given the mission to open their hearts and their lives to those who are broken and living in hopelessness to make known the eternal freedom only found through a relationship with Jesus Christ. To live lives which speak of God's love, redemption, and everything in between. *We are the church!*

As the church, we are called to live unified to fulfill our part completing the mission which Christ has called us to. We may be individuals, but each and every one of us is important.

No other person can fill YOUR shoes! No other person can step in and influence who YOU were created to influence. But we must ALL do it together. All it takes is for us to say YES to the mission. To say YES to partnering with Jesus and reach out to the lost who are in need of a shepherd. To BE the church.

The mercy of God is the game-changer in our lives. When we are aware of the lies of the enemy attempting to blow out our light, we can take action because we have our Father in heaven backing us up as we fully engage in our mission with fresh passion. This is our destiny.

THE CHURCH ISN'T A BUILDING

My first experience with understanding the "corporate calling" of the church was when I was a young child. I went to church every Sunday morning and night and was a part of the church family my whole life. Throughout the week, we gathered together (corporately) and worshiped several times as a church family. If you have never heard the words "corporate" or "calling" in relation to church, don't worry, we will get there. I know to some it may seem like a sort of Christianese or Christian jargon which a lot of people say but don't explain. No worries, I will unpack the meaning .

By the time I was a teenager, I had been to several different churches. Not only did they vary in denomination but also in style and culture. The differences resulted in understanding not *all* churches function corporately. I don't say this to degrade any denomination or church but to shed light on the importance of the church in this world. And in order to fully comprehend this and the function of the church, we have to develop a baseline definition to apply to both words I mentioned. This way we can effectively live it out as ONE church. As the Apostle Paul said:

> ***But now indeed there are many members, yet one body.***
> ***1 Corinthians 12:20 NKJV***

Although there are several churches in existence, according to God, there is only one church--one body of Christ. We may look differently. We may do things a little differently. But we are still ONE. One corporate mission: To see that all people come to know Jesus Christ our Lord.

One of the definitions for the word "corporate" concerns the culture. The dictionary defines it as "shared by all members of a unified group."[5] In other words, the values and purpose of a corporate establishment will be shared by each of its members. They will have the same mission and goal in mind. Even with individualistic personalities, they will pull together to accomplish a singular objective. On the other hand, by definition, a calling is, "a strong inner impulse toward a particular course of action especially when accompanied by conviction of divine influence."[6] Calling defines who we were created to be. This God-created impulse is uniquely designed for whom He destined to fill it. For an individual, this is an exciting discovery that sets us on the path which was once hidden, like the road beneath the Red Sea during the days of Moses. It is now dry ground for us to bravely embarq on. If it is that amazing for an individual, imagine the implications for a whole church! Before we dive into what this means for the church today, let's take a look back to how it was applied to the very first church in the New Testament.

When the people of the New Testament gathered, they did so because they were members of like faith to share in their experiences, as well as the teachings of Jesus. Basically, they were going to church. They had a shared inner catalyst which compelled them toward assembling in unity for the purpose of fulfilling all Jesus commanded. But it didn't just stop there! Not at all! They took what they had learned through gathering and they lived it out. The book of Acts shows us just what it looked like:

So continuing daily with one accord in the temple, and breaking bread from house to house, they ate their food with gladness and simplicity of heart, praising God and having favor with all the people. And the Lord added to the church daily those who were being saved.
Acts 2:46-47 NKJV

They were not just going to church, they were *being* the church! They didn't stop their mission at gathering, they were *praising God and having favor with all the people*. This means they had to actually walk out their calling with others. They corporately lived out their calling as they gathered and when they went out of the temple.

In my earlier days of going to church, the corporate gathering was all I knew about church. Don't get me wrong, I loved this part! It was the setting where gathering together meant each and every person must be unified. I learned early the importance of welcoming the lost and showing them the way to salvation. I learned how to set up chairs, dress modestly, and gather in love with those who believed what I did. Yet, I always felt like something was missing. I knew how *to do* church, but I didn't know how *to be* the church yet.

It seemed I knew a lot of church-going people who gathered corporately were working hard but had no concept of their calling as the church. It was like there was an understanding of function but no application. And often, no joy. Competition and burn-out became the normal atmosphere. It was as if many settled for a "just work until you get to heaven" mentality, rather than an active relationship with the God who created the heavens and the earth. They were like busy insects buzzing about. Ultimately, it was corporate but without calling. Allow me to illustrate my point through a simple lesson of an insect we know of: a honey bee.

God designed all of creation to serve a purpose. The honey bee is no different. Each and every honey bee has a job to do. There is nothing to contemplate, only a task to complete. Each bee does their part without ever asking any questions or doubting their purpose. There is no random honey bee questioning their calling or why they were created. Whether they are drones, workers, or the queen herself, each bee lives and fulfills its purpose.[7] But as children of God, we are created in His image, and for so much more than "just getting the job done." We are in relationship and partnership with the Creator. He wants us to experience the process of changing people's lives with Him. We aren't just His creations, we are His children and co-laborers in His Kingdom!

Here's the point: When we gather together corporately, we partake in only a portion of our relationship with Jesus; when we discover and walk in our calling, on the other hand, we get to live it all out. Sure, we could be Sunday Christians or holiday Christians and have a great time gathering. In fact, in the book of Hebrews, we see how imperative our gathering is:

> *And let us not neglect our meeting together,*
> *as some people do, but encourage one*
> *another, especially now that the day*
> *of his return is drawing near.*
> *Hebrews 10:25*

Gathering together is what makes the church so unique. When we gather, we are agreeing that Jesus is the center of our lives. But regrettably, I feel there are way too many Christians settling for a partial relationship with Christ. They gather and completely miss out on the rest. They overlook the value in the calling.

I discovered during my younger years, many questions began burning in my own heart. Was this the unity Jesus Christ spoke of? Is this what the church was created for? Is the function of the church to just work? I needed to see there was more to this relationship with God than work. I just knew this could not be the sole reason for which we were created or the role the church was destined to fulfill.

In the New Testament, when Jesus entered the scene, what people knew about God and the church received a radical overhaul of perspective. They were confident in the rules they had to follow, the temple they were gathering in, as well as how to worship. But a change was coming! God is and has always been holy. His nature never changes. But, I love how our God is the God of doing new things:

> *For I'm going to do a brand-new thing.*
> *See, I have already begun!*
> *Isaiah 43:19a TLB*

This new thing may have been new to us, but it was orchestrated before the earth was in existence, and this new thing would be done through His Son. When Jesus preached to the people of the New Testament, He was sharing a new concept the people were unfamiliar with. The church, which was spoken of as a *place* of worship in the Old Testament, would now become a *position* of worship. Why? Because He was about to do a *new* thing. I want us to really grasp hold of this! Let's take a journey back to the Old Testament to see what preceded this new shift.

The temple was a place of reverence where the priests selected by God built altars for worship. It was the place where God's presence would fall and His glory would appear (1 Chronicles 22:1). The Old Covenant which God made between Himself and the people of Israel guaranteed His presence in meeting certain conditions. In many places, including Exodus 25, God gave instructions on how to build the temple of worship in which He would dwell among His people:

> **And let them make Me a sanctuary**
> **that I may dwell among them.**
> **According to all that I show you,**
> **that is, the pattern of the tabernacle**
> **and the pattern of all its furnishings,**
> **just so you shall make it.**
> **Exodus 25:8-9 NKJV**

This was the beginning of the church. Their function was to worship the living God of Israel. Preparing the temple was a large part of it. Through obedience, they maintained a relationship with God which was evident to every nation who came into contact with them. But it was the New Covenant which would shift the temple (or church) from being a place *outside* of ourselves, to a place *within* ourselves. We have evidence of this shift through the teachings Jesus gave His disciples.

JESUS SHOOK THINGS UP

The disciples thought Jesus coming as the Messiah meant He would free God's people from government oppression and persecution. I imagine their idea of a kingdom takeover had a wild plan attached, but Jesus was about to shake it up! Scripture reveals the focal point of the radical change was Jesus' arrival and also the positioning of God's children in His Kingdom:

> *And through him God reconciled everything to Himself. He made peace with everything in heaven and on earth by means of Christ's blood on the cross.*
> *Colossians 1:20*

Even though the disciples had one thing in mind, God had a much bigger picture He was bringing to the earth the reconciling of EVERYTHING in heaven and earth. This is a big deal when the disciples gathered together with those they were now called to disciple; it was just the beginning of all God was going to do in the church.

Today in the modern church, gathering is still as vital as it was in the New Testament church. As we discussed, the importance of gathering is only the beginning of what God really intended His people to comprehend. Through Jesus, God's plan was to make us, His people, into the body of Christ, the church. Love is the motivating factor in gathering together (Hebrews 10:24-25)! There is much more God had in mind for His church than simply coming together and being identical in thoughts and actions. Rather, He desired His love be manifested through this setting. There is no healthy corporate setting without love! This is the central aspect of the *position* of worship we discussed: Love. What is another situation which is supposed to have love at its core? Relationship. (We'll talk about this soon).

A heart which is willing to live in a *position* of love manifests God's nature. As we intentionally motivate one another, we will do it well, because of this love. The destination, therefore, will always be good works. Criticism, judgement, and bickering will be like viruses inoculated by our purposeful mission to love people. And because it is our heart's mission, our gifts and talents become highways connecting the lost to our Savior, Jesus Christ.

In Greek, the word for church defined all of those devoted to Jesus as, "followers of Christ who derived their identity and mission from Jesus and understood themselves to be the true eschatological community of God."[8] Essentially, the purpose of this community we belong to is to be the hands and feet of Jesus on earth. Our identity and unified mission comes from being in Jesus, not the things we think we are supposed to be doing for Him. When the power which exists within such a unity functions as God intended, it is a force even hell cannot extinguish! Jesus said it even better to Peter:

> *Now I say to you that you are Peter*
> *(which means 'rock') and upon this rock I will*
> *build my church, and all the powers of*
> *hell will not conquer it.*
> *Matthew 16:18*

The revelation Jesus was making to Peter and the other disciples was something which had never been accomplished on earth before! God had not changed His original plan, but rather, He sent Jesus to live it out. In the verse above, Jesus was revealing the church to be the solid force which hell would never be able to overcome. I want us to understand something. The church which Christ built was no wimpy building! In fact, the church Jesus came to construct on the earth was not a building at all (although our places of worship serve a great purpose for us to gather together). Instead, Jesus came to establish what God had in mind the whole time: *We*, the people of God, *are* the church!

I want you to really take hold of something: We are the living testimonies of all God desires to reveal to the world. We are living foundations through which God's glory is revealed day in and day out. Are you getting it yet? We are living foundations, and our goal is bringing God the glory day in and day out. We are the church built to last eternally with Jesus Himself being the *chief cornerstone*. As Paul said:

> **Together, we are His house, built on the**
> **foundation of the apostles and the prophets.**
> **And the cornerstone is Christ Jesus Himself.**
> **Ephesians 2:20**

To be honest, I believe many of us in the church, to this day, have not fully grasped this concept. Let's dig a little deeper to find the treasure the Holy Spirit desires us to understand concerning God's purpose of the church.

I recently found a treasure in an article discussing the true usage of the term "church" which gave quite a life-changing viewpoint: God's idea of "church" is much different than our own:

> **When Jesus said, "And upon this rock will I build my**
> **CHURCH" (Mt. 16:18), He placed emphasis not**
> **on the word CHURCH, but on the word MY.**
> **The CHURCH is unique, not because**
> **it is called a CHURCH, but because it**
> **is the assembly of believers**
> **who belong to Jesus, who constitute His Body.**[9]

Wow! Did those words sink in? The church is not unique because it is called a church, but because we belong to Jesus! What a shift in mindset from doing to being!

I believe this really expresses the *real* Jesus! He didn't come to this earth to embody a saint with a halo like we see embossed in glass windows in churches around the world. He was much more of a rebel! He came with a mission from heaven to reveal more to us than rules to follow. He came in power and authority. From the very beginning, God's plan was to send Jesus to establish what had been lost in the Garden of Eden: Relationship. Therefore, Jesus's coming was disruption to the system of religion the world was used to. So instead of continuing in a faulty system, it was like He took a hammer and shattered the walls of religion which kept God's people from stepping into the freedom and truth which exists only in relationship *with* Him. His life revealed to the early church how God was more interested in their relationship *with* Him, rather than their performance *for* Him. This revelation shifted the whole foundation of the church. Technically, before the book of Acts, "the church" as we know it did not exist. But Jesus coming established it!

I am certain the greatest revelation which flows from a relationship with God is His love for all of humanity (I told you we'd get to it). Unlike some people, God doesn't pick and choose us to be in relationship with Him based on our merits or special qualities. Rather, His desire for humanity is for not one soul on earth to face eternity in darkness separated from Him, but for all to come to know of the truth and freedom found in Christ:

> *The Lord isn't really being slow about his*
> *promise, as some people think.*
> *No, he is being patient for your sake.*
> *He does not want anyone to be destroyed,*
> *but wants everyone to repent.*
> *2 Peter 3:9*

Therefore, His idea of the church was to reflect this loving relationship us. In this way, the broken, sin-filled world that we live in get and up close and personal look at what love looks like.

Those who have no Father, get an opportunity to come to be loved by the One who will never leave. The sick are healed. Those who find themselves unable to get themselves together, come face to face with the fixer Himself. These miracles take place when we, as the church, place Jesus on display in our lives.

I want to stress something I have learned: what the church of Jesus Christ is *not*. It was never meant to be a place for people to hide behind four walls, but rather be a launching pad to be a church *without* walls. It was never meant to be a place where it becomes commonplace to stand upon platforms and judge those trapped in darkness but be an open altar to those who want to be free. Its purpose was *always* to gather God's people together in unity and worship and to function as the representative body of Jesus Christ (1 Corinthians 12:12)! To be a healing hospital for the hurting seeking refuge, not a holy hotel for those seeking to be exalted above others.

Our mission has always been to function as lighthouses to those who are like ships of brokenness adrift at sea. We are instruments of light because the light of the world Himself lives within us, and by the indwelling of God's Holy Spirit, we are graced to do this very work.We get to show others the light of life: Jesus, through the way we live. They encounter Him through us:

> **Then Jesus spoke to them again, saying,**
> **"I am the light of the world. He who**
> **follows Me shall not walk in darkness,**
> **but have the light of life."**
> **John 8:12 NKJV**

When we are in relationship with the Father, we live a life resembling the life of Jesus. Love is the fruit growing in the garden of a relationship with the Father. Therefore, as we come together as a corporate body, *choosing* to fulfill our calling to love the broken pieces of people like He does, we fulfill what we were put on this earth for.

BE THE CHURCH

I started my first job at the age of 14. I was a freshman in high school and wanted more than my parents had the money for. In order to get the things I desired, I had to get a job. I spent my afternoons after school scooping ice cream. It sounds easy (and tasty I might add), but it was hard work! As I trained, I watched my supervisor make endless combinations without ever looking at a single menu. Mention any combo, and he could do it. Within my first week, I found that not to be the case for me. No matter how many times I read the ingredients for the customer orders, I could not grasp how to make them! By the end of that first week, I was defeated and ready to throw in the towel. I began thinking up ways to tell my parents that I had quit. But I could not let ice cream beat me! I decided to do something I was not good at doing, asking for help! Together, my supervisor and I made those endless amounts of ice cream combinations until we were covered in peanut butter and marshmallows. By the end of that school year, I was an ice cream guru (I can still make a banana split with no hesitation). Teamwork surely got the job done. This is no different in the body of Christ.

The Bible reminds us that God has called us, as the church, to work together to fulfill His mission for people as we have been learning (Hebrews 10:25). This calling is our privilege! As one church, how it looks will not be the same for each and every individual congregation. We have the unique ability to reach those in our sphere of influence with creative and diverse approaches. I believe this is truly representative of the God we serve. He is not in a box. Therefore, neither are we.

Through these distinct means, God has entrusted us to live lives (as a whole body) in ways which reveal how impactful an encounter with Jesus Christ really is. Since we have been grafted into the body of Christ, it is woven within our DNA to see every person we encounter experience the very same freedom. But, we must first learn how to apply this to *our* own lives.

Reaching those we come into contact with has never been about conversion. This has never been our role, but the role of His Spirit (John 6:44). But, this does not leave us without a part to play in God's grand plan to draw all of mankind to Him. Our part comes through us being the church.

Learning to walk in authority and live as Christ did happens through our every day, as we learn to use our gifts to benefit the church when we gather; as well as in our families, our jobs, and even in our communities. This is not *what we do*, but it is *who we are*. We are imitators of Christ (Ephesians 5:1)!

Contrary to what we see in the world around us, Jesus Christ was never simply a fine specimen to model good behavior. Christ is the true example of one fully committed to the God of Abraham, Isaac, and Jacob! The Apostle John, Jesus's dearly beloved, reminds us:

> **Those who say they live in God should
> live their lives as Jesus did.**
> **1 John 2:6**

This reminder speaks volumes to our lives. It speaks not only of our corporate call to go and make disciples of all nations (Matthew 28:19), but it also reveals our individual call to walk in relationship with Jesus and fulfill the destiny God has created for each and every one of us. Because we are called by God to fulfill all of our portion, both corporately and individually, only when we walk in both fully are we truly being the church! I believe Paul expressed this perfectly in his letter to the church of Ephesus:

> *And this is God's plan: Both Gentiles and*
> *Jews who believe the Good News share*
> *equally in the riches inherited by God's children.*
> *Both are part of the same body, and both*
> *enjoy the promise of blessings because*
> *they belong to Christ Jesus. By God's*
> *grace and mighty power, I have been*
> *given the privilege of serving him*
> *by spreading this Good News.*
> *Ephesians 3:6-7*

As God's children we have the *privilege of serving him by spreading this Good News.* Serving God is not a chore, and it should never be seen as something we do to get to heaven. NO! Heaven is our promise; it isn't something we could ever earn by our merits. Being the church of Jesus Christ isn't satisfied by our doing anything, but it is who we are: God's children! And because we belong to Christ Jesus, we actually have the privilege as His kids to walk out our life with Him, just like Adam and Eve (Genesis 3:8). We get to walk in the revelation of all Jesus declared to the people of the New Testament. We don't have to settle for an imaginative relationship, we get the FULL package deal! This is the Good News the world needs to witness active in our lives! Not only did God send Jesus to open the door of Heaven to us, but God reveals this grace through our lives as we live it out in this world:

> *For He raised us from the dead along with*
> *Christ and seated us with Him in the heavenly*
> *realms because we are united with Christ*
> *Jesus. So God can point to us in all future*
> *ages as examples of the incredible wealth*
> *of His grace and kindness toward us,*
> *as shown in all He has done for us who*

are united with Christ Jesus.
Ephesians 2:6-7

I really want us to get the depths of these two verses. So let me share it with you in the Amplified Version to help us get just a little bit more:

And He raised us up together with Him
[when we believed], and seated us with
Him in the heavenly places, [because we are] in
Christ Jesus, [and He did this] so that in the
ages to come He might [clearly] show the
immeasurable and unsurpassed riches
of His grace in [His] kindness toward us
in Christ Jesus [by providing for our redemption].

Did we catch this? Through *the ages to come*, He desires to reveal the Good News of Christ through *us!* Talk about a partnership! Cory Asbury hit it out of the park with the chorus in one of my favorite songs, "Reckless Love." In the song, he speaks of how our God will do whatever it takes to win our hearts. He gave everything to have it![10]

When we make the decision to be the church God always intended us to be, we will walk in reckless abandonment because we will understand with our whole being it has never been about anything we have done or not done. We will understand we were once lost sheep running loose in the wilderness of this world, yet He didn't stop until we were safely in His care. We will see through the eyes of our Father who desires to reveal this love to the world around us. We will understand our every word and action are opportunities to display His radical saving love without question.

Just as our Father never gave up on us, we can never give up on others or on ourselves. There were times in my own life that I knew

I was supposed to be loving people, but some people are SO hard to love. I was kind, and it wasn't returned. I've given 110%, only for there to be no reciprocation. And no matter how hard I tried, until I truly grasped God's powerful love, I never could truly love another person well. But when I realized God loved me no matter what I did, I was then better able to love other people no matter what they did. This was life-changing for me. Thankfully, the truth of God's word frees us from anything contrary to His plan for us. We are the church because of all God has done through Jesus. This isn't just a fancy phrase said to make us feel good. It is everlasting truth!

Maybe you feel like you are new to this revelation, but *you are* the church! Maybe you are wondering if it is too late to jump in the saddle and live it out in your life. Guess what!? It isn't too late! I love how Amber Olafsson said it in her book *THE AWESOME ONE* when sharing her journey about being the church:

> *"I think a lot, if not all of Christ followers start*
> *off our journey with the Lord with child-like*
> *faith—in awe of what He has done*
> *and the forgiveness we've received...*
> *I remember feeling like someone had*
> *lit a blazing bonfire in my soul... But somewhere*
> *along my journey, my focus shifted from*
> *what Christ had done to what I was doing...*
> *I was no longer simply receiving the gift*
> *of salvation, but striving to earn and*
> *sustain God's favor in my life..."*[11]

I am confident many of us can relate to feeling as if somewhere along our journey, we have become less like blazing fires and more like dimly lit sparks needing a rekindling. We've got some good news! As long as we have breath in our bodies, we have the opportunity to walk in absolute freedom. We have the opportunity to be a bright shining light to those in darkness. We have the opportunity to be an influencer for every single person we meet. The fire in us was lit at salvation; it is not out completely. It may feel like we are only a flicker, but our God can light what seems dim:

God Himself is Fire!
Hebrews 12:29 MSG

So what do we say? Are we ready to be stirred? Because the time is now. It is time for us to burn bright...

6

STOKE THE FLAME

Sometimes, life just seems to happen. Sure, we have ups and downs every single day. We even have to face the natural consequences of things (even if we may not want to admit it). But, there are also seasons of life which are a whole other experience, where things happen beyond our control. Yet, even in the midst of those times, I have learned NOTHING is beyond God's control.

Up to this point, I have shared about our purpose and mission as God's children and how our enemy would like nothing more than to put out the fire within us which thrusts us forward into completing the work we are each called to. Now, I want to share a bit of my story with you. I know all too well what it feels like to have the fire in your soul feel at danger of going out completely. I know all too well what it feels like for circumstances to overwhelm the light within you making your mission seem difficult and almost impossible!

To be completely transparent, the story I am about to share has radically changed me. I will never again be who I was before my journey. Like some of you, I have been in a place where I questioned if I could stand firm on God's promises when the mountain in front doesn't seem like it will move. I have stood, legs shaking in exhaustion, as I walked through the challenge which tested my faith beyond what I thought I could handle. And I have held tight, hands feeling insecure and weak, to the promised land which lies ahead because the God of the universe is my Father who is always faithful! Travel with me, as I share a journey which forever challenged my understanding of the transformation power of trials. I now have a new understanding of this passage:

> *These trials will show that your faith is genuine. It is being tested as fire tests and purifies gold—though your faith is far more precious than mere gold. So when your faith remains strong through many trials, it will bring you much praise and glory and honor on the day when Jesus Christ is revealed to the whole world.*
> *1 Peter 1:7*

Have you ever sat in a church service, or listened to a song on the radio, and you just knew the message was about you? One Sunday at my own church, this was exactly what I experienced. I heard a sermon which revealed exactly what I had been going through for a six month period; not just for me, but for my family also. Through all I had gone through, we learned as a family, faith is truly built in the fire. And everything we knew to be normal would change us forever...

MY STORY

Six months prior to this life-altering church service, everything changed. It was the day before Mother's Day in 2017, and I was hit with pain worse than I ever thought possible on the left side of my face. I hadn't done anything weird to cause it. It literally appeared out of nowhere! As if some faulty switch in my brain was flicked on, this pain invaded my life like an unwelcome guest.

The level and intensity of the pain was difficult to grasp or even understand. The only way I can explain it would be comparing it to getting teeth pulled with no medication, while holding a blow-dryer, and standing in a lightning storm. On a pain scale of one to ten, it was more like a twenty! For the record, I have never actually experienced any of these scenarios, but like I said, it was very intense. It was enough pain to bring this tough Army mom who birthed four kiddos to my knees. And every single day, without warning, I continued to experience shocks, numbing, and searing pain. With tears streaming down my face with every jolt, I came to the realization: Life as I had known it was completely *interrupted!*

In search of relief, I visited three doctors over a twenty-four hour period. And each time, I found no answers or relief. With every new prescription, I discovered nothing I was given could touch the pain boring into my face. I prayed. I cried out to God. And still, there was pain. My interruption was yet to be solved.

Finally, after three days of torment (and trying to "be" strong), I just had to do something. There was this persistent feeling deep inside that something was not right. I knew then that I needed to do something about it. I couldn't just wait it out. I needed to act. I decided to take a chance and make an appointment with my dentist. I am truly thankful God gives us His Holy Spirit to tug at our stubborn hearts which sometimes serve to prolong the arrival of the answers we are crying out for:

When the Spirit of truth comes, He will guide
you into all the truth, for He will not speak on His
own authority, but whatever He hears He will speak,

and He will declare to you the things that are to come.
John 16:13 ESV

After (patiently) seeing my dentist five times the following week, I found some answers. Not all. But some. He was able to rule out some definite concerns and discovered some possibilities of what "might" be taking place. Thankfully, he prescribed me something to lower my pain. Unfortunately, it would be months before I could see who I really needed to, a neurologist. This meant more months of limited answers and results. I don't know about you, but I like surety and confidence when things are not right. The question I sometimes ask myself is: What if I had not listened to the Holy Spirit when He led me to keep being seen? What would have happened if I'd given up and just dealt with my suffering? I am confident I would not be where I am today.

Over the six-month span, I had several attacks a day. About twenty-five at the least. Even with a temporary medication to take the edge off, I still was not at 100%. I was barely at 50%. I was hardly surviving each day. I waited. Praying. But still in pain. Minimal emotions, isolation, and fatigue were some of the side effects of my medication. And still things did not get better. Not yet. Every now and then, they actually got worse! Weather changes, ceiling fans, and even a simple brush of my cheek, among other things, sent me into a tailspin of excruciating pain. All of the things which were once harmless seemed to drown me in fear of impending attacks. Soon, fear and anxiety began to knock at the door of my heart, threatening to steal my peace and my faith; all that which was stable within me was completely shaken. At this point, I questioned if my faith was strong enough to endure this.

The pain I lived was completely physical, at least at first. It affected the way I ate, the way I spoke, and limited my ability to smile. I was becoming consumed by it, and I definitely felt trapped in my inner battle. Yet, I continued to pray. But at times of increased pain, I held onto the smallest bit of hope that God was nearby. I held onto the smallest fraction of faith I had while I was struggling to see the light at the end of this tunnel. As my composure unraveled, I grasped and held to His promise:

> *Faith shows the reality of what we hope for;*
> *it is the evidence of things we cannot see.*
> *Hebrews 11:1*

Right in the middle of my battle, my life did not pause. I am pretty confident if life could pause, we probably wouldn't learn the lessons of true hope and faith. I think it's in the collision of our planned-out life and the interruptions we experience where God does His best work. He doesn't need us to struggle to grow, but I believe it's in those moments when He is really able to capture our attention and affections. He is able to take hold of our trembling hands and broken hearts and reveal just how much of a good Father He really is!

As a Christian, I felt like I was failing in one of the greatest battles I had ever faced. How was I going to appear to those who were looking up to me?! I was a "leader." Leaders are supposed to be automatically healed and always be okay! People *depended on me* for hope. They *depended on me* to encourage them, yet what I really felt was maybe I missed a memo somewhere? I believed in healing, and I even prayed healing over others, but *my* pain wasn't going away! This invader and unwelcome entity was becoming mine and was shifting my reality. I had begun to wear it as a garment. I began to live as if I was in a glass box, anticipating the future shattering of my whole world. I felt like I could no longer trust my thoughts or my faith. I was in a mental prison which almost seemed to outweigh the horrendous pain I was in. Yet, somewhere within my spirit, I knew my God had not left. And if I knew nothing else, I knew God was, is, and will always be faithful:

> *"I am the Alpha and the Omega—the beginning*
> *and the end," says the Lord God. "I am the*
> *one who is, who always was,*
> *and who is still to come—the Almighty One."*
> *Revelation 1:8*

He met me right where I was, in my weakness. He was not afraid of my pain or my doubt and He did not shrink back when my faith wavered and my heart failed. What a God!

I got honest about the battle I was going through. On some days, I couldn't remember the names of those I knew. There were times when I could not finish a thought because I had to choose medication over mental clarity. Even in the midst of all the struggle, I knew I had to trust my Heavenly Father. As I shared my trial with those close, they prayed. They encouraged. They filled in the gaps of the areas I could not control in my weakness. But indeed there was something I was still missing: hope.

One day, the Holy Spirit spoke something which began to break the glass surrounding my mind. Time and time again, people prayed healing for me. Over and over they approached the throne room of Heaven and pleaded for it all to disappear. I liked the sound of those prayers, but the Holy Spirit challenged me to pray something else. He whispered something life altering to my heart:

> *"Do not spend time praying any longer for*
> *healing. The healing is done. Pray for the*
> *courage to stand in the storm."*

A shift took place in my soul. I was praying for something I had already obtained through all Jesus had done on the cross. I was not living from a resurrected life but from a broken one. He revealed in the midst of the pain, I had started losing sight of my identity in His Son. He reminded me of who I truly was:

A chosen generation, a royal priesthood, a holy
nation, His own special people, that you may
proclaim the praises of Him who called you
out of darkness into His marvelous light.
1 Peter 2:9 NKJV

The shift in my prayers set me on a path to not only acknowledge I was healed, *but live like I was healed.*

After six months of debilitating pain, I learned to draw closer to God than ever before. My family learned to serve one another because most days I was limited and required rest. It was an experience which stretched my entire family. It reminded me afresh that wherever I went, God was close. Whatever I thought, He was present. Whatever I felt, He knew. Even when the pain was drowning out my thoughts and I felt like I would shatter under the pressure, I could shout, "God, you are my healer!" Even when I didn't "feel" healed, I could whisper, "Father, you are faithful!" I learned regardless of what I felt or saw, He was still faithful to His word. Regardless of the weakness I was weighted under, He was my joy and my strength.

SHAKE OFF THE FEAR

I have often thought motherhood is similar to being a superhero in more ways than one. Notice I said "similar to" because being a superhero is for the movies, not real life. Anyways, I never expected helping my children combat fear would be one of those ways. Fear shows up in the lives of my four children in ways just as diverse as their individual personalities. For some kids, fear can drive them to leap into danger because they would rather face it head on than run from it (at least one of my children displays this kind of gumption). But for some children, fear can be debilitating and feel life threatening. For one of my children in particular, the latter was the result.

I learned pretty quickly fear was hanging around when one of my usually brave kiddos was in utter anguish at bedtime. When the end of the day had finally come, shutting the lights off at night became a "not so smooth" process. The very idea of knowing darkness was in the future caused a lot of scary thoughts and fear-driven behavior. At least four nightlights were plugged in every night as part of the regular night-time routine. Let's not forget the millions of hugs and kisses to seal the deal of comfort. Comparable to my experience of feeling trapped in the physical and mental anguish associated with the pain I was experiencing which led me to an unhealthy mindset of fear, my child was also in need of a change. A shift in mindset was in fact necessary. Fear was unwelcome and needed to go!

After my husband and I prayed, we knew this was a readjustment our child would need not just for bedtime but for their whole entire life! During our daily sit downs and nightly prayer time with our family, we spent a lot of time speaking to all of our children concerning fear. We got vulnerable and each took precious time to expose the lies which fear had whispered to our hearts. I also shared about the special weapon my own mother passed on to me: The Mighty Name of Jesus:

> *Therefore, God elevated him to the place of highest*
> *honor and gave him the name above all other names,*
> *that at the name of Jesus every knee should bow,*
> *in heaven and on earth and under the earth,*
> *and every tongue declare that Jesus Christ is*
> *Lord, to the glory of God the Father.*
> *Philippians 2:9-11*

All of our children needed to know how powerful the name of Jesus is not just the one afraid of the dark. It was essential they understood and experienced the power of the name of Jesus to which every knee bows! We desired for our children to witness the tangible power of Jesus which kept them safe in the dark, as well as the pain from consuming me. The fear of the dark may not seem harmful in itself, but it is. I believe once fear is allowed to remain, no matter what it may appear to be in the life of an individual, it will stay. As it stays, it will multiply until it consumes every area of safety within the hearts of people. Unfortunately, fear is often one of the most accepted mindsets not only in the world but in the church. I honestly don't believe it is done out of sheer welcome, but out of tolerance because it can seem to be easier. You see, my child felt as if they could just have the comforts they needed; they could deal with the fear in a way which seemed manageable. But is this how God has called us to deal with fear? Absolutely not! The Bible actually tells us *not* to fear:

Such love has no fear, because perfect love expels all fear.
1 John 4:18a

If fear were something we were ever meant to manage in our lives, then God's word would have said so. But, it does not. Instead we find as we keep reading further in 1 John 4, there is a vaccine which defends us against fear: Love! Yes, there goes this word again! Love is not just a fuzzy feeling. Love is the very character of God. Love overcomes fear because it destroys the seeds fear sows in our hearts. Fear tells us we are not enough. Fear tells us we have to earn God's love. Fear tells us God is too far away to reach us. And like it did with my child, fear can sometimes lead us to feel like we have to grow into comfort with it. But love expels every single one of those lies!

Wonder why we are confronting the issue of fear? Because fear is not harmless, and if not confronted, it will stay. Fear consumes and destroys. Fear delays and it cripples minds. Fear twists and distorts truth. And the greatest reason why we must confront fear?

Because God did not give it to us:

For God gave us a spirit not of fear but of power
and love and self-control.
2 Timothy 1:7 ESV, emphasis added

As children of God, our relationship with Him is completely rooted in trust. Fear is the absolute opposite of trust. Our trusting relationship with God is based solely upon who He is, not on what we do or don't do. If we allow fear to settle in our hearts, then we can slowly lose trust in God because of our temporary circumstances. Sure, our circumstances can feel consuming to us, but God is greater than any of our circumstances. He is God! And if He said it, then He is faithful to His word! As He spoke to the prophet Isaiah:

Remember the former things of old, For I am
God, and there is no other; I am God, and there is
none like Me, Declaring the end from the beginning,
And from ancient times things that are not yet
done, Saying, 'My counsel shall stand,
And I will do all My pleasure.'
Isaiah 46:9-10 NKJV

LIVING IT OUT

So, how do we live lives on fire for the mission God has called us to, in the center of the valley and wilderness seasons of our lives? How can we possibly be a light to anyone when our own light feels in danger of going out completely? By faith. Because by faith, we are able to stand firm, even when it is hard to make sense of anything around us.

We are not alone but have been preceded by many whom stood strong in their faith as adversity loomed and death lurked. Yet, they stood because the God we serve is faithful. The God who spoke light into existence is the same God who breathed life into Adam. The same God who delivered the children of Israel out of slavery is the same God who emboldened David to defeat Goliath. The same God who prepared Noah for the flood before water fell from the sky was the same God who made Abraham the father of many nations. And the same God is ALIVE in me and in you!

What we face cannot withstand the God who was, is, and is to come (Revelation 1:8). Those who died standing firm in faith were not left empty but were fulfilled by a graceful and merciful God, and so, we also stand firm in our faith:

> **Let us hold fast the confession of our hope without wavering, for He who promised is faithful.**
> **Hebrews 10:23 NKJV**

Remember my story of pain I shared with you? Well, my perspective of things did not stay the same. In the middle of the greatest fight of my life, I was presented with a choice: drown in my circumstance or follow Christ and speak to my storm. Because of Jesus, I could not remain in my mindset of fear and anxiety. I had to choose faith instead. It wasn't just my life that was at stake but every single person I encounter. Faith in Jesus is an anchor; it gives us hope and boldness regardless of our trial (2 Corinthians 3:12).

Have you ever noticed in the middle of a storm, the sun peeks through, and then suddenly, things start to seem calm? For a moment, it seems the storm, which had been unrelenting, was completely dissolved in a matter of minutes. In life, it can feel like the weight of everything we have been holding in during a storm finally gives, and we can breathe for the first time. Right before my highly anticipated neurological appointment, something shifted and changed within me. All of the weight I had been carrying for so long was lighter. My thoughts were lighter. My whole countenance was lifted. The pain was still around, but it no longer owned me. For the first time, I had come to truly understand what the Apostle Paul was speaking about in 2 Corinthians 4.

The Apostle Paul was a man who suffered severely for the gospel. But in spite of all he went through, he considered his troubles to be "small" and not lasting "very long" compared to the weight of eternity:

> *For our present troubles are small and won't*
> *last very long. Yet they produce for us a glory*
> *that vastly outweighs them and will last forever!*
> *So we don't look at the troubles we can see now;*
> *rather, we fix our gaze on things that cannot be*
> *seen. For the things we see now will soon be gone,*
> *but the things we cannot see will last forever.*
> *2 Corinthians 4:17-18*

The only way to truly consider such intense struggles as small would be to compare them to the weight of eternal glory which is in our future. The Apostle Paul understood this. I came to understand it. I believe the only way to comprehend something as unseen as eternity is by experiencing the love of God.

When we have a true encounter with God's love, we come to see ourselves the way that He does. It becomes impossible to view our struggles as anything less than opportunities for His glory to be revealed. We become less like trick candles that go in and out with a minor gust of wind but more steady and constant, the way He always destined us to be! When all you know is shaken, the fire within you is at risk of burning out completely; you feel like your soul is at the brink of death and are completely undone. This is when we can encounter the breath of God which breathes new life into us. His life. His strength. His grace. His courage. His love.

The Lord is near to those who have a broken heart,
And saves such as have a contrite spirit.
Psalm 34:18 NKJV

My broken and fragmented heart had a collision with its Maker as He reminded my soul He was not finished with me yet. I knew what God was doing was a brand new thing. He was remaking me. Filling me anew. Refreshing things which were dry, and blowing on the embers which were barely lit.

If all this life-altering remaking was not enough, right before my anticipated appointment, the pain began to subside. It had gone down to a manageable level. I was feeling relief. God continued to work in me to break the glass surrounding my mind from the previous six months. You see, shifting and changing are a process. As God shifts things within us, He is like a careful surgeon who delicately removes harmful things and leave all the good. In my case, those dead things were thoughts and behaviors which had become a part of who I was. And only a good God and loving Father could remove such deeply rooted pain with precision and perfection.

During my season of shifting, God continued to speak healing over me. He brought songs to my spirit. He led me to His word. He even led other people to me to speak words which would eventually alter me forever. My pastor was one of those people. He spoke words which were like a defibrillator to a heart void of life:

> *"If you do not take your thoughts captive, they will take you captive!"*[12]

Words can be like cancer to an already fractured heart. The many words of encouragement and words of prayer filled my soul to overflowing, but those words from my pastor seemed to make my world go still! Something in me cracked. The glass around my mind, which was crippling me from seeing the truth, broke and shattered like a window being smashed to pieces from a violent storm. Not only was my mind free, but I could feel the freedom in my body as well! And I was able to recognize the turning point within myself.

Fast forward to my neurological visit. The neurologist ran every test he possibly could to determine the depths of what I was dealing with. He took several in depth x-rays, ran a CT scan, and did several neurological pain tests. All of which seemed almost pointless that particular day because I had been medication free for a month by my visit! But, what was more freeing was my mind, which had once been imprisoned in glass to pain but now had become a new fortress built by the very words of God. Were things back to normal? Around my home, yes. But I was forever changed. Who I was before my storm was gone. I was made completely new because:

"On the other side of your trial, is your miracle."[13]

I have no idea what you may be going through in your life. I may never experience the storms you may be walking through. But, I know one thing for sure, my God is the same God who is walking through your storm with you. I may not understand your trial, but He does. And what He has done in and through me is what He can do in and through you. But, there is one thing required of you just as there was one of me, FAITH:

But without faith it is impossible to please Him, for he who comes to God must believe that He is, and that He is a rewarder of those who diligently seek Him.
Hebrews 11:6 NKJV

Unless we have faith, we will never be able to do all God has purposed for us to do. Without faith, we will never be able to withstand the storms. Without faith, we will not be able to trust a faithful God during unrelenting chaos. Faith isn't just for us to get what we want. Faith is to get us through the hell which bursts into our comfortable lives.

Faith is the comfort of our soul when we have no answers for the pain. Faith is the command for the mountain consuming our minds to MOVE! Faith stokes the fires which are at risk of going out because of what we may be going through. As Banning Liebscher said in his book *Rooted*:

> **"Asking what you desire and seeing God do it for you is called faith."**[14]

If we claim to believe, then we must not stand back and become storm watchers anticipating to be overtaken by the tornado of death sucking up our life. We must decide for ourselves, nothing will stop us from being exactly who God has created us to be. We must make the decision, nothing on this earth deserves a seat on the throne of our heart. Not pain. Not sorrow. Not people. Not things. Absolutely nothing can separate us from the love of a Father who gave everything for relationship with us. Absolutely nothing.

PART THREE

A burning flame gives light "to all who are in the house" (Matthew 5:15 NKJV). We are to live as lights in this world. When we are ablaze, we must remain ablaze. In this part of the book, we will learn to hold tight to the fire now burning inside for the sake of the Gospel. We will also look at practical ways to advance the Kingdom of God in our lives boldly and for His glory.

7

ADVANCE

What is the first thing that comes to mind when you think of pursuing purpose? To some, it may be achieving their wildest dreams. While others, it may be simply being able to have money left over after pay day. For some, it may be traveling to foreign lands. Others may wish to step outside their front door for the first time without fear. It will always look different to each and every person. However, one similarity remains: It is the intentional act of working hard toward something we are really passionate about. In order to walk in our purpose, we must be intentional to pursue it by taking the leap to transition from where we are, to where we are supposed to be. Purpose and transition cannot be separated. They work together. Without moving forward, purpose remains elusive.

I love being a mother. It has not always been easy. There were seasons fraught with difficulty when I questioned if maybe God made a mistake. He didn't just bless me with one kiddo but four! I've sometimes wondered if perhaps He miscounted when he gave all those kiddos to me. I never felt worthy of them. Sometimes, if I am honest, I still don't. But little did I know, God had a purpose for my life. I am so thankful being a mother was a wonderful portion of His great plan:

> *For my thoughts are not your thoughts,*
> *neither are your ways my ways, declares the Lord.*
> *For as the heavens are higher than the earth,*
> *so are my ways higher than your ways*
> *and my thoughts than your thoughts.*
> *Isaiah 55:8-9 ESV*

As a mother, I find the most exciting yet difficult time is watching my children transition. From one period to the next, I find myself longing for the current stage to end while simultaneously holding onto it. Basically, I want the impossible! I want my children to both grow up into thriving adults and stay little and need me forever. I want them to get married and have families of their own. At the same time, I want them to sit with me and play Go-Fish until someone eventually quits! But if I want them to reach their purpose, I have to not only let them transition, but I have to be willing to transition too! Transition must happen. It is life. It is the power which propels transition to move us forward into our destiny. It is this forward movement our God desires us to come into. To move ahead, to fulfill the mission. And in this, we recognize and resist the stumbling blocks keeping us from becoming who we are called to be.

The Bible tells us God has created each of us with a unique purpose. It is written in our DNA to walk in it. Bu,t we all know living in this world can drown our vision with negative views and unrealistic expectations of what our purpose should look like in our lives.

It is our purpose which repels the tendency for us to stay in our current stages of life, while transition reminds us to keep moving forward. We can't continue to struggle with the longing to grow while wishing for things to stay the same. We must pursue what God has called us to: People. And just as a seed does not delay itself from bringing forth its kind, God desires we do not delay our future any longer but we transition into the destinies awaiting each of us.

When we look all around, it doesn't take much to see the world is offering a million ways to find our purpose. In relationships. In money. In careers. In wants. In hobbies. None of these things are bad! They are a normal part of our lives. God gave us desires for a reason! But, when we allow the world to define our purpose based on these things, it hands us opportunities to compare ourselves and even question our effectiveness and worth. And in this place, the enemy of our soul is there to cloud our minds. Satan is a liar and tries to get us to believe God must have forgotten about us, because:

The thief's purpose is to steal and kill and destroy.
John 10:10a

How often has the enemy come to steal our purpose? If we really take a moment and pinpoint those instances, perhaps they didn't feel as wild as a storm, but could have been subtle like a passing shadow. We may have noticed the chaos first, but the enemy's plan for destruction began in the seeds planted in our hearts long before the chaos was born. Think for a moment, have we ever felt like our friends are perfect and don't make as many mistakes like we do? Or our leaders are definitely more gifted than we'll ever be? How about the old friend on Facebook? They seem to have it all together, don't they?! Or maybe comparison isn't the stumbling block. So instead, Satan attempts to make us focus inward. Our thoughts start overflowing with doubts and rejection. Our minds become bombarded with a wrecking ball of emotions. We begin feeling unwelcome or unappreciated, and our hearts break from not being invited—a feeling of just not ever being able to measure up.

But today my friends, enough is enough! It is time to recognize the thief who has been slowly blowing out the fire of your soul. It is time to leave the insecurities, the broken heart, and the feelings of not being enough at the feet of Jesus. It is time to leave comparison at the cross. It is time to shut the enemy up and stop him from stealing any longer. It is time to look in the mirror and truly see who Jesus says we are.

My heart is so stirred because I believe in this season, God is challenging us to not just pursue our purpose in *our hearts* but to step out courageously and *walk* in the purpose He has for us! He is awakening us as a body. He is inviting each and every one of us to a deeper place with Him, where we can exchange our *feelings* of not being enough with the *truth*, where we as a people no longer wear garments of insecurity or low self-worth, but instead wear security and self- confidence ....

Before this day, you may not have known it, but God thinks highly of you! And not only does He have a purpose for your life, but He desires to reveal His purpose to you:

> ***And we know that God causes everything to work***
> ***together for the good of those who love God***
> ***and are called according to his purpose for them.***
> ***Romans 8:28***

His purpose for your life are the same truths which God declared over the Israelites in their time of great struggle:

> ***"For I know the plans I have for you," says the***
> ***Lord. "They are plans for good and not***
> ***for disaster, to give you a future and a hope."***
> ***Jeremiah 29:11***

But, we must be willing! Only when we become willing to transition from our past, whatever it may be, into our purpose will we become who we were meant to be: the fully functional Body of Christ. The church is incomplete if we, the children of the King, don't step into our rightful place. The Apostle Paul said it best:

> *All of you together are Christ's body, and each*
> *of you is a part of it.*
> *1 Corinthians 12:27*

Concerning the working of each of us together to create a whole, he said:

> *He makes the whole body fit together perfectly.*
> *As each part does its own special work,*
> *it helps the other parts grow, so that the whole*
> *body is healthy and growing and full of love.*
> *Ephesians 4:16*

Here is a truth I believe the Father desires each of us to grasp: Our lives will be a testimony of who we believe we are and a representation of who or what governs our life. In other words, the words we speak and lives we live will ultimately reveal what is most important in our lives. Either it will be Jesus or something else.

The world around us awaits true intimacy with a loving Father, even if they don't know it yet. And our lives are the beacon of hope through which He is revealed. The world is waiting on us to walk in our God-given purpose to reveal Him. When we transition into our true identity, then we will walk in our purpose simply because we know who we are and whose we are. An identity fully realized in Christ is like a fire, no matter what winds may come to snuff it out, it cannot be extinguished.

So, who do you believe you are? What is your identity rooted in? When people come into contact with you, what testimony is your life declaring? I am not talking about what inspirational messages you post on your social media or what Jesus t-shirt you are wearing. The t-shirt or cool bracelet may turn heads, but is it turning hearts? What I am talking about is who people say we are on our toughest days when it looks like there is no hope, and what people believe we stand on when we have been wronged by another. As children of God, we were chosen to fulfill a destiny authored by God Himself. I love how Lisa Bevere said it in her book *Without Rival*:

> *"You were a kidnapped heir who has been ransomed. One of the most glorious, courageous things you will ever do is to live in the fullness of all that the death of Jesus purchases for you."*[15]

Regardless of the lies which have been spoken over you, you are not a mistake. You may have made mistakes, but your mistakes don't define God or the destiny He has placed in your soul. Neither have your mistakes caught Him off guard. You have not ruined His plans or changed His mind. You are not without purpose. How do I know? Because His word says so:

> *But you are not like that, for you are a chosen people. You are royal priests, a holy nation, God's very own possession. As a result, you can show others the goodness of God, for he called you out of the darkness into his wonderful light.*
> *1 Peter 2:9*

When we walk in purpose, we become like intricate parts of a timepiece. Each and every part plays its unique role. And when we do, we are walking in purpose! This life isn't only about us.

Yes, we each have individual gifts and calls upon our lives! But, it is much bigger than just us! We were designed to work together to reach those who are lost in darkness. Most people look at an analog clock and see only the time. They see only what is most visible. You could choose just to see the time on the clock. Or, you could choose to see it requires all the inner pieces to make the outer pieces function properly, for everything to work together so the clock can serve its purpose, telling us what time it is. This is what it means to be a part of the Body of Christ!

Regardless of what lies the enemy has placed in your heart up to this point, it isn't over. God is not finished with you. You are not alone, and it's not too late to get started. The only way for the body of Christ to function effectively is to walk in our purpose to fulfill the mission *together*. This can only happen if *you* are the *you* God created *you* to be. We, as the Body of Christ, need you to be you. The world needs you to be you.

Before we move on any further in this book, I believe God is wanting us to really grab hold of who He says we are. He desires us to rise up and transition from the place of complacency, insecurity, and fear, and transition into our purpose. Today is the day to expose the enemy's lies. Maybe he's telling us we have no purpose, or our identity is found in the cares of this world, or we have to work for God's love. Why do we need to confront these lies? Because when we expose the liar, we shine the light into dark places, and the liar can no longer hide. Our enemy can no longer be a threat!

Our identity as God's children is what gives us **purpose** to fulfill the destiny He created us each for. As it says in 1 Corinthians 12:12:

> *The human body has many parts, but the many*
> *parts make up one whole body.*
> *So it is with the body of Christ.*

We each have a role to play. And so, we must move forward and transition into our purpose. The world is in desperate need of it.

MOVE FORWARD

God has this way of grabbing your attention in the most creative of ways. On one day in particular, He did just that. As I was praying, the Holy Spirit placed a very interesting word in my mind that I wouldn't have thought of in my regular day to day: Squatters. "Squatters? Are you for real, God?" I blurted out loud. I don't know about you, but out of all of my conversations with God, this was definitely a first. He definitely has creative ways to draw us in to sit and listen. As I sat and listened to the path He was taking me down with this word, He began to connect the dots piece by piece.

The Holy Spirit led me to look into the definition of what a squatter is. It is defined in one of two ways (depending on the situation):

A) One that settles on property without right or title or payment of rent

B) One that settles on public land under government regulation with the purpose of acquiring title[16]

Basically, they are people occupying a property which they have not paid for. They take up residence on the property without every acquiring the means to pay for it fair and square. In my state of North Carolina, this is called the Doctrine of Adverse Possession. According to this law, the squatter is able to openly possess a title which they do not own. However, the squatter must do so openly for twenty years before they can file for a title to own the property. If there is a "color claim" meaning the squatters may "believe" they own the rights to the property, then the opportunity to obtain rights decreases from twenty years to seven years, offering them an opportunity to file for a title. Even state owned properties can be subject to adverse possession.[17]

What God began to reveal blew my mind! The biggest squatter within the territory of the church has been Satan! He knows he has no rights to our territory. But, he knows if we don't lay claim to it by our rightful inheritance, he will own the territory. This is what he has done and continues to do. He squats because we either don't know our territory or we don't lay claim to it. This is how darkness spreads! It squats where we don't step in and possess it. But. it's time to kick the squatter out and possess the land which our Father has given us authority over!

We see Satan attempt to pull the scheme on Jesus in Matthew 4. As Satan offered Jesus the opportunity to align with him, Jesus stood upon the Word. Jesus knew His identity was in the Father, not in what Satan offered. What Satan didn't know was Jesus was about to take the keys to the Kingdom back!

I want us to truly grasp this: When sin entered this world, identity rooted in relationship with the Father was lost. This loss allowed Satan to squat where we—as children of God—were given dominion. But by the sacrifice of Jesus Christ on the cross, dominion was restored (Revelation 12:11)! Satan was defeated! And he still is!

A truth we each must face is this: If we have no identity, we cannot transition into our purpose! Our enemy knows whether we know our identity or not. If we don't know who we are, Satan doesn't technically need to stop us from walking into our purpose because we do it ourselves. Hosea 4:6 reminds us that a lack of knowledge equals destruction! We must walk upon the foundation of our inheritance through Christ:

Furthermore, because we are united with Christ,

we have received an inheritance from God,
for He chose us in advance, and He
makes everything work out according to His plan.
Ephesians 1:11

This is where our identity is rooted. This is who we are. This is who God says we are. God sees us as those on whom He has bestowed an inheritance. He sees us as whom He has called us to be, not who we think we are. He sees us for the great destiny which He has purposed for us. He sees us as part of His body.

We must be willing to acknowledge that maybe we have allowed our enemy to make us focus inward, on our struggles, our pain, our depression, and so, we have not been able to see what's in front of us. And, what's before us is a mission and a mandate to be liberators, to be lights in the darkness, to be the ones who possess the key to freedom? Jesus!

We must abandon living below our means as children of God, for the righteous are bold as lions (Proverbs 28:1). A relationship with Christ is full of life and freedom and should not consist of struggle or begging to earn His grace and mercy. Those things can't be earned, neither can you struggle to have them. We are seated with Christ:

For He raised us from the dead along with Christ
and seated us with Him in the heavenly realms
because we are united with Christ Jesus.
Ephesians 2:6

We are inheritors. Not from our acts but because of His Son's. We have God's favor; we don't need to earn it. This would make Him a bargainer. He owes no man (Romans 11:35). Rather, He is our Father. The Creator of the universe, who spoke all of creation into existence, has taken residence inside us. We are children of the

King.

So the questions we must then begin to ask ourselves are these: How do we transition from brokenness to identity? From lack to purpose? From past failure to future possession? *MOVE FORWARD.*

1. WALK THROUGH THE DOOR. When we fully accept our identity is in Christ, then we are able to accept the inheritance which Christ died to give us. We are able to walk from being an orphan in religion to a child in relationship:

> *How blessed is God! And what a blessing He is!*
> *He's the Father of our Master, Jesus Christ, and*
> *takes us to the high places of blessing in Him.*
> *Long before He laid down earth's foundations,*
> *He had us in mind, had settled on us as the*
> *focus of his love, to be made whole and*
> *holy by His love. Long, long ago He decided*
> *to adopt us into His family through Jesus*
> *Christ. (What pleasure he took in planning this!)*
> *He wanted us to enter into the celebration of His*
> *lavish gift-giving by the hand of His beloved Son.*
> *Ephesians 1:3-6 MSG*

2. CLOSE THE DOOR TO PAST FEARS AND WALK INTO OUR NOW PURPOSE. No more allowing the squatters of darkness steal from us what is ours by inheritance! God has a purpose for us NOW. It isn't lost or hidden. It is time to stop hurting ourselves and calling it comfort. It is time to be free:

> *But to all who believed Him and accepted him,*
> *He gave the <u>right</u> to become children of God.*

They are <u>reborn</u>—not with a physical birth
resulting from human passion or plan, but a
<u>birth that comes from God</u>.
John 1:12-13, emphasis added

3. STAND UPON THE TRUTH. Even when we don't feel like it, we are still who God says we are. We are the children of God who have been given the keys to the Kingdom of Heaven. Let's walk in our divine purpose:

And I will give you the keys of the Kingdom
of Heaven. Whatever you forbid on earth will be
forbidden in heaven, and whatever you permit
on earth will be permitted in heaven.
Matthew 16:19

8

FINISH STRONG

Our two youngest boys love to play outside. Their favorite game is digging (definitely not conducive to a beautiful yard). No matter how many times that I give them "the talk" about not digging in the yard, I often find them stick and rock in hand, bulldozing away. One afternoon I decided to walk over and see what all the fun was about. I figured if they were that bold to bore into their Dad's beautiful grass, they must have a reason. "Hey, what are you digging for?" I asked. Startled and caught in the act, our youngest yells out, "Fossils." At this point, I was curious. I couldn't comprehend why they thought they would find fossils on a golf course, but I asked anyway, "What kind of fossils?" They both smiled. I think at this point, they thought I had forgotten about the fact that they were breaking the rules. Instead, both boys beamed a big grin and shouted, "Dinosaur fossils!" They stood up and started telling me all about the pride and joy that they were sure was there. Both were beside themself in sheer delight! They were confident that all that they had to do was keep digging. It was worth it to them to find what made their heart happy. Their imagination was overflowing with excitement and wonder. Even if the sun stopped shining and the rain started to fall, nothing could hinder the bliss that had captured their hearts for what lay hidden as treasure in the dirt. The faith my boys had for those dinosaur fossils could not be shaken. Their belief may have been rooted in childhood awe, but it reveals so much of how God created each and every one of us.

We were created to live in the same curiosity and child-like faith that my boys have (Matthew 18:3). Their belief in what they had not yet seen was firm and unshakable. The seed of possibility growing within their hearts held them fixed on what is possible rather than menaced by what may seem impossible. This same seed lives in us my friends! A gift that is given supernaturally. A faith that is not intimidated by the rains of life that threaten to run us away and abandon our destiny to discover the awesome path that He lays before each of us. Our lives are meant to be the testimony of His fingerprint on each page of our story. God designed us with the exact same ability to be anchored in faith in all that He is and all that He can do in our lives. Jesus said that when He is the treasure, we listen and follow, our lives a firm no matter what comes:

> *It is like a person building a house who digs*
> *deep and lays the foundation on solid rock.*
> *When the floodwaters rise and break against*
> *that house, it stands firm because it is well built.*
> *Luke 6:48*

What if we could be so firm that circumstances could not break us, like a house built on the rock? Nothing could stop my boys, rain or shine, from completing their mission. THE GREAT NEWS: There is nothing we can ever face which can keep us from fulfilling what God has created us for! Nothing we face can threaten to snuff out the burning blaze within our souls or defeat us. Why? Because the God inside of us is much greater than the adversity around us:

You are of God, little children, and have overcome
them, because He who is in you is greater than
He who is in the world.
1 John 4:4 NKJV

Because we know the One inside us is greater than our enemy, we can face the challenge to move in and occupy much greater territory than we have in the past. Let's rise up and walk in the authority of Jesus Christ for the expansion of the Kingdom of God and scatter the darkness in this world with the light of life, burning bright within us! I challenge us to MOVE FORWARD. Because, if we ever expect to recover the territory the enemy of our soul has occupied, then we must choose to step into areas which intimidate us, challenge our theology, and stir the fire within our very soul. If our hope is to accomplish the mission of seeing every person we encounter liberated from the kingdom of darkness and restored into right relationship with the Father, then we must take the risk of living dangerously by faith.

When we choose to live by faith in such a way it threatens the plans of our enemy, we better believe he will stop at nothing to keep us from fulfilling our mission. He will attempt to hinder us by throwing up roadblocks along our path to interfere with our progressive move toward the place God has called us. This is the reality of what we stand against. This is the war in which we are engaged. The war is not physical like the ones our brave military forces face every day, but it is between the Kingdom of God and the kingdoms of our enemy:

For our struggle is not against flesh and blood
[contending only with physical opponents], but against
the rulers, against the powers, against the world forces of
this [present] darkness, against the spiritual forces of
wickedness in the heavenly (supernatural) places.
Ephesians 6:12 AMP

What I have come to learn is even in the midst of the most challenging of seasons, God is present. There is no battle we face against our enemy where God will be absent. There is no depth where our God cannot reach us. There is no wall our God will not kick down to restore us. No matter what we have been through in our past, He is still present. He is still faithful. He cannot fail. When we feel in danger of the light in us burning out, He is faithful to blow upon those embers. In their powerful song, "Do It Again," Elevation Worship reminds us of this truth: God's faithfulness is never ending. I can depend on it because I can depend on Him. This is our Father![18]

What we believe about God and His ability to walk through hard wilderness seasons with us will ultimately define us, our thoughts and behaviors, and affect those around us. We will either burn brighter because we have rested in the presence of the Almighty, or we will shrink back—our light having been snuffed out by fear. Yet, the opportunity remains for us to look like what we have been through! By faith, we have the opportunity to reflect the God we have clung to in the good and the bad. I believe Kris Vallotton expressed this best:

> *"Whomever God is to you that is what He will be through you."*[19]

The story I shared of the personal storm I was walking through is still not over in the natural. It is finished in the spirit, because I choose to live by the Biblical principle of Matthew 6:10: "...[it] (meaning God's will)be done on earth as it is in heaven!" But, I still have to walk it. Some days, I experience no pain at all, and I feel completely uninhibited and ready to climb Mount Everest (not really). And some days, the pain appears, and I must rest and remind my soul, it is *already* finished! Because, I am a child of the God who created all things by His voice, which:

Calls those things which do not exist as though they did.
Romans 4:17b NKJV

After all I have experienced in this life, I have made the courageous choice to only move forward. To not settle for being dimly lit but to remain on fire. Storms will come, but so will the sun. Valleys of shadows of death will surround me, but He resides inside me. I can no longer go back to who I was before I was altered. Just as a person cannot go back into their mother's womb, neither can someone who has experienced new, deep intimacy with God go back to their prior relationship with Him. I have gained scars through this battle, but what I have also abundantly gained is the knowledge of God's grace and love when I was at my lowest. When we gain but a glimpse of the God who makes us new, we are forever changed. We are forever in pursuit of the depths of His heart for us. One of my favorite authors, A.W. Tozer, articulated this thought so perfectly:

> ***"In Christ and by Christ, God affects complete
> self-disclosure, although He shows Himself
> not to reason but to faith and love. Faith
> is an organ of knowledge, and love an
> organ of experience. God came to us in
> the incarnation; in atonement He reconciled
> us to Himself, and by faith and love we
> enter and lay hold on Him."*** [20]

In Christ, we are whole and complete. Through faith and love, God continually draws us to Himself. Even when the scars we earn in battle threaten to leave us incomplete and battered, we serve a God who mends, who regenerates, and who makes all things new (Revelation 21:5). We only need to BURN BRIGHT.

God's plan from before time has always been relationship and intimacy with His creation. His desire is for us to not only *experience* Him but for us to *enjoy* the intimacy as well. It is an absolute joy to be in His presence! In His company, we are filled, no matter what the condition of the fire is within us. His love is bottomless. Abner Suarez opened my eyes to this area with a revelatory statement:

> *"It's hard to hunger for something you've never tasted. One great paradigm shift that the Holy Spirit longs to reveal is the absolute joy and pleasure experiencing God. We were designed and created for divine encounter. Our joy is found in the experience of knowing Him. Unfortunately, many who know the joy of salvation remain ignorant of the joy that comes from walking in their salvation. The ability to know Him is available to every person. The joy of continuous encounter with God is not an obligation or something He forces upon His followers. He simply extends an invitation of love and waits for us to respond."*[21]

When we get to the place where we desire His presence more than anything, we position ourselves to remain in a steadfast place of receiving from Him and experiencing all He is. Burning bright becomes a natural consequence of being with the Father. No circumstance, care of the world, or devil in hell could hinder the illumination which will shine through us when we have chosen to abandon the past hindrances of this temporal world for the sake of the gospel. This is what we were created for!

BE THE LIGHT

Have you ever felt unqualified? On my blog at *Fiercely Silent*, I shared on this relevant topic because most people (including myself at times) often feel like this.[22] In this particular post, I share about how these feelings limit what God desires to do in and through us. Why? Because if we are only focused on who we believe we are in the eyes of other people, we cannot stay focused on our mission.

As much as we would like to avoid the journey we are on, we can't. When we realize God uses all things in our journey for good, we wouldn't try to so hard to run from the hard things we face. Instead, we would run toward them knowing what they produce in us:

> *My brethren, count it all joy when you fall into*
> *various trials, knowing that the testing of*
> *your faith produces patience. But let patience*
> *have its perfect work, that you may*
> *be perfect and complete, lacking nothing.*
> *James 1:2-4 NKJV*

Our youngest child is probably our most adventurous. Even before he could walk or talk, he always managed to find adventure. He would hide and beg me to come find him (not fun in a clothing store). Every time I take him to Lowe's, he gives me a million reasons why he needs another flashlight. I am convinced it is not so much the adventures he finds with flashlights, but he genuinely **loves** light! I mean, he turns on every single light he passes, even in daylight, simply because he believes we always need **more** light in our lives (of course, my husband does NOT appreciate light in this way). He was wired to enjoy everything around him being bright! This is simply the way he was created. The truth is, this is how God wired each of us.

God originally designed us to be children of light, and the whole world would shine bright because of who we are and because we belong to the Father of lights. This is our destiny. Christ has restored our position which was lost in the garden, empowering us to now walk as bright lights to continue the work the Father started in the beginning.

The Bible shows us in passage after passage of Scripture of our destiny to shine:

> *Let your light so shine before men, that they may see*
> *your good works and glorify your Father in heaven.*
> *Matthew 5:16 NKJV*

> *Then the righteous will shine forth as the*
> *sun in the kingdom of their Father.*
> *Matthew 13:43a NKJV*

> *But if we walk in the light as He is in the light,*
> *we have fellowship with one another, and*
> *the blood of Jesus Christ His Son*
> *cleanses us from all sin.*
> *1 John 1:7 NKJV*

Like my little lover of the light, we were created to shine so brightly the darkness around us flees. Just as darkness cannot stay when someone turns on a light in a dark room, neither can darkness remain when we burn bright as vessels of God's love.

Let's not run from our journey any longer, whether it is filled to the brim with accomplishments or it isn't. God is looking for those who will be ministers of reconciliation in this world (2 Corinthians 5:18-21). He is looking for those who are willing to stand in the trenches with the broken. For those unconcerned with comfort and ready for the mission at hand.

The beautiful thing is, our unique journey will serve a particular purpose in this world. Whatever it may be, don't hide it! Allow God to use it, for His glory! It is time to be **REIGNITED** for the Kingdom:

> *You are the light of the world. A city that is set*
> *on a hill cannot be hidden.*
> *Matthew 5:14 NKJV*

Conclusion

I wholeheartedly believe when we, as the full Body of Christ, begin to be on fire for the Kingdom, the world around us will be able to witness the love of God in full action. Often, we allow the negatives we experience in life stop us from walking in all God has for us. If we fully grasped the gravity of the purpose God has placed inside of us, we would never allow ourselves to reach the place of burnout.

When I wrote my first book *In Pursuit of Purpose*, God was already watering the seeds in my heart for the message in this book. As I sat putting the finishing touches on the very first book, He spoke something over my heart which took a year to understand, *"You will live this one."* Those words then were full of authority, but I had not connected with the power behind them yet. I could not imagine I would face the greatest battle of my life to date. I had not comprehended He would become my portion in a way I had not known before. I did not expect He would show me how close I could get to burning out but remain ablaze because His word was deep within me.

As I began putting each and every chapter together in this book, God continued to reveal each element. Piece-by-piece, I was given a deeper and deeper revelation of the message He desired to speak to the hearts of His people. One thing you learn when you write a book, or preach a message, is your life is always the litmus test of your belief system. Every element I wrote about, I experienced. At times, I felt as if I was failing. Other times, I felt as though I was succeeding. And the times in between, I attempted to disconnect my life from the message. Even in my attempt to mold the theme at times, He was merciful to lead me to *His* message. Our God is much greater than our misconceptions and failures.

As I finished the final chapter, God brought massive revelation to my life. As a people, our lives are often the only gospel others ever come into contact with. How we live and respond to God becomes almost like a beam either drawing people toward God or pushing them away from Him. In my case, the pain I have experienced for the last year revealed a God who gives strength and grace during very difficult seasons. As I clung to God, He continued to reveal His faithfulness. And I hope every person I encountered, encountered Him.

As I shared, each element was revealed by God in pieces. Have you ever had someone give you a gift which was wrapped inside of a small box, then placed inside of a larger box, placed inside of another larger box, and on and on? This was exactly what it was like! It was like experiencing continual revelation persistently adding layers onto this message. Don't mistake what I am saying. He was not trying to play a cruel trick on me or anything! He is a good Father. Rather, He was drawing me in to pursue the message intentionally.

Remember the massive revelation I mentioned? Well, it concerned a very specific element of the book which tied every piece together: Eight. Yes, as in the number! God was about to reveal what the number eight had anything to do with my book and my life. He was about to reveal what He was doing in me and through me during one of the hardest years of my family's life.

As you have seen (it's ok to go ahead and check), this book has eight chapters. As much as I tried, I did not feel like God was leading me to go beyond this. Even as He was revealing new elements to each chapter, I still felt like eight chapters was the max. Then, He revealed how the number eight was intertwined with my life. Allow me to lay it out for you.

Numbers hold symbolic meaning in many cultures, and the cultures of the Bible are no different. In the Bible, numbers take on both a symbolic as well as literal meaning. From Daniel to Revelation, numbers are used in a definite pattern.[23]

The number eight specifically holds meaning in the Bible because it signifies "new beginnings." In my own life, it has represented absolute newness; I am not who I was before my journey. In the Bible, there are several passages of Scripture which reveal a pattern of significance with the number eight.

Circumcision took place on the eighth day, and it symbolized total submission to God. As we know, circumcision was a covenant relationship between God and His people which began a rich heritage of a people dedicated to the Lord:

From generation to generation, every male child must
be circumcised on the eighth day after his birth.
This applies not only to members of your family
but also to the servants born in your household
and the foreign-born servants whom you have purchased.
Genesis 17:12

Noah and his family were the only survivors during the flood (eight in total). Humanity would begin anew, and Noah and his family would be the beginning:

> *And God did not spare the ancient world—except for Noah and the seven others in his family. Noah warned the world of God's righteous judgment. So God protected Noah when he destroyed the world of ungodly people with a vast flood.*
> *2 Peter 2:5*

In order to atone for sin as well as dedication to the Lord, sacrifices were required. Therefore, the sacrifice of the first-born was also on the eighth day:

> *And the Lord said to Moses, "When a calf or lamb or goat is born, it must be left with its mother for seven days. From the eighth day on, it will be acceptable as a special gift to the Lord.*
> *Leviticus 22:26-27*

The process of sanctification is also linked to eight days:

> *They began the work in early spring, on the first day of the New Year, and in eight days they had reached the entry room of the Lord's Temple.*
> *Then they purified the Temple of the Lord itself, which took another eight days. So the entire task was completed in sixteen days.*
> *2 Chronicles 29:17*

This obviously does not exhaust the list of the usage of the number eight, but let me show you where I am going with this.

In my own life, the number eight has revealed resurrection and absolute regeneration! Who I was before my storm was not a "bad" person. But, who I am now is the person God needed me to be for the next season of my life. Had I chosen to shrink back in the face of adversity, I would not have written the words you are reading now. Had I trusted my feelings of inadequacy, fear, anxiety, and every other feeling, I would have missed the opportunities of growth. Did I get it right every single time? No. But I chose to trust Him and just enjoy the ride.

If I can leave you with anything, it is this: Your life is a beacon of hope. You may not feel like it is all the time. Maybe nobody has ever cared enough to tell you. But guess what, God thinks so. He loves you, and He has given everything to reveal this love to you, and then through you, to the world. God's mission for humanity is for them to come to know Him as He truly is, through the filter of His love, not through the filter of our brokenness. Our lives are His filter of love.

The Bible tells us we should "desire to prophesy" (1 Corinthians 14:39). When we do, we reveal the very heart of God for His people. God desires for us to reveal His heart, not just through our words, but through our lives. As we focus on the mission He has called us to, we will remain ablaze and draw those who are lost, to the Father who is waiting for their return. And so, I want to prophesy over you...

I declare, in Jesus's name, your life will be a vessel of hope and love. The world will come to know the Father's heart through you. I speak courage and boldness like a lion over you as you stand in the storms of life, trusting in the faithfulness of our God. You WILL be all which God has created you for. You WILL fulfill the mission to love people as God loves people. You WILL burn bright. You ARE REIGNITED. AMEN.

NOTES

1. Merriam-Webster Online, s.v. "Re," Accessed June 27, 2018, https://www.merriam-webster.com/dictionary/re.

2. Merriam-Webster Online, s.v. "Ignite," Accessed June 27, 2018, https://www.merriam-webster.com/dictionary/ignite.

3. Gangel, Kenneth, O. "John, vol. 4." Holman New Testament Commentary. Nashville, TN: Broadman & Holman Publishers, 2000.

4. Merriam-Webster Online, s.v. "Financing," Accessed June 19, 2018, https://www.merriam-webster.com/dictionary/financing.

5. Your Dictionary Online, s.v. "Corporate," Accessed August 16th, 2018, http://www.yourdictionary.com/corporate.

6. Merriam-Webster Online, s.v. "Calling," Accessed June 20, 2018, https://www.merriam-webster.com/dictionary/calling.

7. "Inside and Out of the Beehive." Perfect Bee. 2018. https://www.perfectbee.com/learn-about-bees/the-life-of-bees/inside-and-out-of-the-beehive/.

8. Greever, Joshua M. "Church." The Lexham Bible Dictionary, edited by John D. Barry et al. Bellingham, WA: Lexham Press, 2016.

9. Duffield, Guy P., and Nathaniel M. Van Cleave. Foundations of Pentecostal Theology. Los Angeles, CA: L.I.F.E. Bible College, 1983.

10. Asbury, Cory. "Reckless Love." By Caleb Culver, Cory Asbury and Ran Jackson, Produced by Jason Ingram and Paul Mabury. Recorded September 2017. Track 1 on Reckless Love. Bethel Music. Digital download and streaming.

11. Olafsson, Amber. The Awesome One. North Carolina: UNITED HOUSE Publishing, 2018.

12. Brice, Al. "Faith." Faith Conference, Covenant Love Church, Fayetteville, NC, October 2017.

13. Brice, Cameron. "You Have What It Takes". Covenant Love Church, Fayetteville, NC, March 2018.

14. Liebscher, Banning. Rooted. Colorado Springs, CO: WaterBrook, May 3, 2016.

15. Bevere, Lisa. Without Rival. Grand Rapids, MI: Revell, August 16, 2016.

16. Merriam-Webster Online, s.v."Squatter," Accessed September 5, 2018, https://www.merriam-webster.com/dictionary/squatter.

17. "North Carolina Adverse Possession Laws," FindLaw Online, 2018, https://statelaws.findlaw.com/north-carolina-law/north-carolina-adverse-possession-laws.html.

18. Elevation Worship. "Do It Again." By Mack Brock, Chris Brown, Matt Redman and Steven Furtick, Produced by Mack Brock, Aaron Robertson, Seth Mosley, Mike "X" O'Connor. Recorded September 9–21, 2016. Track 3 on There is a Cloud. Provident Label Group. Digital Download.

19. Vallotton, Kris. "Core Values of the Prophetic." July 10, 2018, in Kris Vallotton's, podcast, https://krisvallotton.com/core-values-of-the-prophetic/.

20. Tozer, A.W. The Knowledge of the Holy. New York, NY: Harper Collins, 1961.

21. Suarez, Abner. Creation Reborn. Maricopa, AZ: XP Publishing, 2014.

22. Tubbs, Natasha. "We Are All Qualified." Fiercely Silent (blog). September 1, 2018. https://fiercelysilent.com/blog/2017/11/6/we-are-all-qualified.

23. Elwell, Walter A., and Barry J. Beitzel. "Numbers and Numerology." Baker Encyclopedia of the Bible. Grand Rapids, MI: Baker Book House, 1988.

ACKNOWLEDGEMENTS

To my husband, Caron, thank you for being the rushing waters to my fiery heart. Your love, support, and open arms offer me peace and sanctuary.

To my children, Tyler, Nadia, CJ, and Kai, your zeal and passion remind me of how wealthy I am. Thank you for challenging me to be the mother God created me to be.

To my tribe, Amanda and Tasha, you girls are like the side-mirrors in my life. You watch my blind spots as you continually uphold me in prayer and fill me with laughter. You girls make life the joy it was always intended to be.

To my publisher and fire-sister, Amber, you have radically stirred the fire in my soul to keep writing when I wanted to quit. Your coaching has stretched me in my craft and challenged me to be the writer God has created me to be. Your friendship reminds me that God is so good.

To the entire UNITED HOUSE team, you all have worked hours perfecting this work. Thank you from the bottom of my heart.

To my Pastors, Al and Tava, your faithfulness to live by the words you preach have grown me tremendously as a disciple of Jesus Christ. Only a loving Heavenly Father could have known that we needed such loving shepherds to lead our family.

To my leader, Pastor David, you have stretched me beyond my comfort zone for the sake of what God has planted deep in my soul. Thank you for every opportunity to stir the gifts of the Spirit. Your mentorship as a spiritual father has led me to see the Father's heart for those He loves.

To all of those who have helped launch this work, thank you for all of your love and support during the season of writing these words. This book would not be possible without you.

About The Author

Natasha is a Christian Counselor certified by the Board of Christian Professional & Pastoral Counselors. She received her M.A. in Pastoral Counseling and her M.Div. Theology from Liberty University. She currently trains and equips Prophetic Students in her home church's School of Ministry. Her first self- published book, *In Pursuit of Purpose*, has become a beacon of hope as it challenges God's people to walk in their God-given purpose and pursue true relationship with Jesus. As a teacher, she is passionate about connecting people to the heart of the Father and leading them to become all God has created them to be. She is a huge New England Patriots fan, tea drinker, chicken wing expert, and lover of the ocean. She, her husband, and their four children are currently stationed in North Carolina as an Army family with their two dogs.

You can learn more about Natasha on her blog
or sign up to receive her free newsletter at:
NatashaTubbs.com

OTHER BOOKS BY NATASHA TUBBS

In Pursuit of Purpose

*Available at Amazon.com

CPSIA information can be obtained
at www.ICGtesting.com
Printed in the USA
FFHW020619290919
55264040-61007FF

9 781732 719460